An American Hostage in Iraq

Nabil Seyam's Journey from Captivity Under Saddam to Living the American Dream in America's Heartland

by

Nabil Seyam, Ph.D.

authorHOUSE™

1663 LIBERTY DRIVE, SUITE 200
BLOOMINGTON, INDIANA 47403
(800) 839-8640
WWW.AUTHORHOUSE.COM

First published by AuthorHouse 09/08/04

ISBN: 1-4184-8508-X (sc)

Printed in the United States of America
Bloomington, Indiana

This book is printed on acid-free paper.

Dedication

To my parents who made all the difference in my life

Biography

Dr. Nabil Seyam is director of the Board of Administration of the Islamic Society of Wichita and co-founder of the Annoor Islamic School. He performs Friday sermons, marriage and divorce ceremonies, and death sermons. Dr. Seyam conducts marriage counseling and provides countless activities for Muslims and people of other faiths. He has done more than 300 speeches and interviews on politics, religion, peace-building, and multiculturalism throughout the state of Kansas. He was the recipient of the Leader of the Year in 2002 in Wichita and most recently was the recipient of the Community Servant Award by the University United Methodist Church in 2003. Dr. Seyam was selected for the Community Servant Award because of his active role in peace-building and multiculturalism throughout Kansas.

Dr. Seyam received his undergraduate degree in industrial engineering from Wichita State University and his master's and Ph.D. in safety engineering from Kennedy University. He is an adjunct instructor for Pittsburg State University and Wichita State University. He is certified as a Professional Environmental Auditor and an Ergonomic Evaluator Specialist.

Dr. Seyam had and is still serving on many boards as an advisor, including those of the American Society of Safety Engineers, Pittsburg State University, Wichita State University, Newman University, Inter-Faith Ministries, Global Learning Center, Mayor Knight's diversity task force, the Child Care Association, International Society of Martial Artists, etc. His monthly writing on Islam is featured in the Q&A Times, and he has hosted a popular television series called ZYGO on public television station KPTS.

Besides his occupation as a corporate health and safety director and expert in the field of ergonomics, Dr. Seyam has been interviewed by reporters from CBS, ABC, NBC, radio stations and newspapers here and abroad about his perspective on such issues as politics and religion.

Dr. Seyam's personal relationship with many government officials (city, county, state, the governor, FBI, prisons, Highway Patrol.) has helped enhance the reputation of the Muslim community of Wichita. Recently has been selected by the leaders of Wichita to serve on the Visioneering Wichita Steering Committee. He is married and has six children.

Preface

Nabil Seyam grew up in a poor Palestinian home in Kuwait, dreaming one day of studying and getting a good job to support his family. His life was faring well. After graduating from Wichita State University, where he married his first wife, Carrie, the two moved back to Kuwait to start a family.

Seyam was a safety engineer for a successful pipe manufacturer. Carrie taught at an American school.

Then Iraq invaded Kuwait in 1990. Like many others at the time, Seyam lost his job. He and his family went into survival mode, selling eggs outside mosques and driving as far as Basra, Iraq, to sell electronics. His family, being Palestinian, passed through the checkpoints the Iraqis had set up across Kuwait. Seyam, being a Palestinian-American, knew he was at risk. Other Americans were being detained. Some were arrested and taken to strategic locations as "human shields."

Two months after the invasion, Seyam didn't make it past a checkpoint. He was arrested, beaten, and bused to Baghdad, where he was among a group of 25 captives.

They spent 15 days in a hotel that the military had turned into a headquarters for operations. International pressure helped free Seyam, but the experience left him nearly penniless and jobless. The captivity kept him from seeing the birth of his third child, who was with Carrie in Wichita.

The U.S. Embassy paid for his flight to Wichita, where he started over. He and his family bought groceries with food stamps. He got odd jobs at temp agencies. He fought to get his life back.

Now, he is the corporate director of health and safety for an international company, overseeing many plants. He lives in an upscale neighborhood on a golf course. But his new life is more than just a corporate success story.

He and others founded Wichita's largest gathering place for Muslims, the Muslim Community Center. He founded the city's first Muslim school. And he's served a vital role as spokesman for the estimated 5,000 Muslims in the central Kansas community, especially since the terrorist attacks of Sept. 11, 2001. Within an hour of that tragedy, he decided to issue statements to the local media, emphasizing the sorrow the Islamic community felt and how their beliefs differed sharply from the terrorists' hypocritical version of Islam.

He has spoken in churches, schools, colleges, and community centers across Kansas. He still speaks today for a variety of groups sharing his perspective. The job of informing the world about true Islam is never done, he has said.

His story of triumph over captivity is unusual because he was the rare Arab-American taken hostage during the first Gulf War. His story of returning to the United States, rebuilding his life as an executive and as a leader in the Muslim community in the nation's heartland is more than just an American dream realized. He did this in a city where Christianity is the dominant faith.

He has seen Iraqis who claim to be Muslim but violate its laws by drinking and caring more for Saddam's philosophy of conquest than the Qur'an's mandates for moral living and building peace and justice.

His perspective of the occupation of Iraq by the Bush administration and the role of Arab leaders for the past 56 years is a unique one.

Contents

Chapter 1

My father and his entire family were expelled from Palestine in 1948. They found refuge in Jordan until 1957, when my father had an opportunity to move to Kuwait, which was not yet an independent state. My father worked as a tailor and struggled as a foreigner in an Arab and Muslim land. In 1960, my father married a lovely Lebanese woman who also came from a poor family. My mother always told me, her first-born: "You were the first candle which lights our home."

When my brothers and I were young, we did not have toys or games like other households. We made guns and toys out of wood and paper.

My first memory of a struggle is when my father tried to enroll me in a government school. He was told, "You and your son are foreigners. You must enroll him either in a private or in a Palestinian afternoon school." My father had no choice but to enroll me in a Palestinian afternoon school, one that met after the regular government school was over.

One of the best blessings was having Palestinian teachers who affected my entire life. They were tough on us and treated us like their own kids. Education to Palestinians is like a weapon — you can always use it anywhere you go. Teachers used to hit

First grade

1

us with wooden sticks, because they wanted us to be the best. They cared about us, about our families, and about our future. Although at that moment I hated many of them, I can see now that they were the reason for my success today.

Although the cost of the tuition was only $24 a year per student, my father was unable to pay it. The situation was even worse when three of us (brothers) went to the same school. I recall the administrator calling our names in the afternoon roll call. Students who did not pay the tuition were forced to stand in front of the entire school to be expelled. To prevent the expulsion and humiliation, our mother would borrow the tuition from close neighbors, and my father would pay it off within a year. My brothers and I walked to school daily in the stream hot of Kuwait for at least an hour. By the time we arrived to school we were sweaty and tired. Government students would go to school from 7 a.m. to 1:30 p.m.; we would go to school from 2 p.m. to 8:30 p.m.

During recess, many of our friends would buy sandwiches, but my brothers and I would just sit and watch. As we got older, my father would give each of us an allowance to buy soda pop and a cheese sandwich. Our economic situation was bad enough that my mother would make rice and yogurt for dinner, and we would eat the same meal two days in a row.

Palestinians shared the same schools but different times, teachers and administration. The bathrooms of the school used by the morning kids were so filthy that we would not even use them.

Although I came from a devoted family, Islam was practiced more as a culture than a religion. I recall that at age 10, I would line up all of my brothers and sisters to pray behind me. I would also call upon my parents to join us. I was very fascinated by hearing the recitation of the Holy Qur'an by some of the most famous Egyptian recitors. While in middle school, I joined the Jamaa Islameiah (Islamic Group) at age 14 to learn more about Islam. Within the group, we were taught humbleness, Qur'an recitation, and how to be good believers and obedient to God. The teacher would always ask me to lead the prayers in his absence. During school recess, the school administration would play loud music and songs to the point it was annoying and, some of us thought, non-Islamic. But a group consisting of myself and others was able to convert most activities in the middle school so that they more closely reflected Islamic values. The group consisted of teenagers who were the smartest in the school.

By the time I was in my senior year of high school, I had five sisters and four brothers. Being the oldest is not fun, since you have to set an example for all of your brothers and sisters. Our families put so much pressure on the oldest to carry the responsibility and to help parents in old age.

My family lived in a Palestinian neighborhood in Kuwait. The Kuwaitis had their own areas and villas, and we (foreigners) had our own areas, cities and schools. They received free education, transportation, and uniforms, but we paid for our own education, transportation, and uniforms. The foreigners and the Kuwaitis neither associated nor assimilated.

The 12 of us lived in a two-bedroom apartment with one bathroom. We had bunk beds all over the place, in addition to blankets being laid on the floor at night. My father had no driver's license and never owned a car because he couldn't afford one. It was very unusual for us to travel or go anywhere. When we needed to visit a relative, we called a hatchback taxi and crammed everyone into it. My mother would call each of our names to make sure all 10 kids were in the taxi. I will never forget the time when we forgot my brother in the neighborhood; he was two years old. After we driven for more than 20 minutes, my mother realized he was missing.

Our breakfast was the best in the world: My mother would save the old, hard pita bread and cut it into small pieces and dump it into hot tea. Fried eggs, white cheese, and olives were considered a fancy breakfast. We always ate all the meals together, with the whole family eating from the same steel dish

At age 13, I discovered I was a good soccer goalie. Practicing on the sand and playing daily had made me a very good player — not just in the neighborhood, but outside the city, too. Many teams would ask me to play for them, but not a Kuwaiti team. I tried but was told, "You are not a Kuwaiti citizen, therefore, you cannot practice or play for a Kuwaiti team." So I joined a Palestinian team and became their main goalkeeper.

Soccer team

At 14, I decided to start taking karate lessons. Karate and soccer were too much for my mother and father to accept. In fact, I was allowed only two hours a week of sports, but I used to play secretly.

I was the only karate student who did not have a karate suit, because my father was unable to afford one. I saved all of my allowance for a whole year and bought my first karate suit. By 18, I was a black belt in karate and one of the best goalkeepers in the country.

Karate

To support the family, every summer I would work for two months and give all my income to my father. During the school year, my brothers and I would help my father in the tailoring business, and in the summer I would work for others for minimum wage.

Life in high school is totally different than middle school. It is harder, tiring and more serious. Your entire future is determined in that stage. Since the high school was about 15 miles away, we had to pay a private bus driver to pick us up daily. On the days the driver did not show up, we had to walk 15 miles in the heat of Kuwait. By the time we got to school, we were exhausted and sweaty and had missed much of the school day. But we never thought of skipping

5

classes, because missing class for any reason including sickness might mean failing the year. Graduating from high school is a major accomplishment overseas. Education there is totally different than here in America. By the time we graduated from high school, we already had taken calculus 1, 2, and 3, differential equations, biology 1 & 2, physics 1 & 2, chemistry 1 & 2, English or French, and many other disciplines. If you flunk one course, you would repeat the entire year and all the courses over again. Studying for the final examination in high school is a stress that cannot be described. If a student fails, the whole family fails. Two moments I will never forget occurred in my last year of high school: We won the soccer tournament, and I acted in a play before the school principal.

Being a Palestinian living in Kuwait is a disadvantage when it comes to college and building your future. Kuwait University has very strict rules of admission that are designed to limit the number of foreign students.

A Kuwaiti can enroll in Kuwait University with a high school grade of 48 percent or higher, but a foreigner has to have 80 percent or higher just to fill out an application. A foreigner with a 95 percent grade is not guaranteed to study what he or she wants. The university dictates what to study to pressure you to leave and go somewhere else. If you enroll in another country in the Middle East, your grade will be reduced by 10 percent. For this and many other reasons, foreigners in Kuwait were not happy, but due to economic reasons the majority of people had no choice but to stay.

Palestinians are not like other foreigners. If others are deported, they can go to their homelands. But Palestinians are immigrants, foreigners, and nationless anywhere they go. As Palestinians, we had no future unless we had a college degree. So looking for a university to accept me was a priority. I sent copies of my certificates to India, Pakistan, and Iraq.

Since Iraq is a short distance from Kuwait, I decided to travel to Baghdad with two other classmates. That was my first independent travel outside of Kuwait. After three days of struggle in Baghdad, going back and forth, we were told that "the only way we can accept you as Palestinian students is through enrolling in the Baath Party." At age 18, we knew no politics nor how good or bad the Baath Party was, so we declined the request. I was very disappointed that the admission was based on politics. Walking in the streets of Baghdad looking for a room in a hotel to sleep was more than an experience. As soon as I asked for a room, the attendant would say, "no rooms." A little after dark a Palestinian attendant said, "Yes we have rooms." I said, "I have been searching for a room for hours, why there are no rooms in the hotels?" He said, "You look like an Egyptian, and the relationship between Iraq and Egypt is tense; therefore many attendants refused to give you a room." A few days later we headed back to Kuwait. Heading back with my mission unaccomplished was very disappointing. Since I was the oldest in my family, I knew I could do something to bring my family out of poverty, but no one was giving me the chance. Although I was under a lot of stress, I knew myself, that I was a fighter and one day would make it.

My father suggested that I start working and concentrate on where to go in the future. I started as a timekeeper for Kuwait National Industries. There, I met many Palestinian men who had sent their sons and daughters to the United Sates. The idea hit me. Without my parents' knowledge, I went to an office in Kuwait City that specialized in obtaining college admissions. After three months, I received admission to Pittsburg State University around July 1980. I'd selected faraway Kansas because it offered the programs I desired and because tuition was low.

The next step was the hardest. I had to stand before a U.S. Embassy representative and pass the screening test, where questions were asked about what the student intended to study, whether they planned to stay in the United States after graduating, and so on. Each day there were dozens of applicants, but only one or two would make it. Finally, I told my family about the plan of going to America. Surely, the plan was firmly rejected. "America is too far, how are you going to live, who is going to make your food, who is going to wash your clothes …?" my father would say. After a week of deep debate, he said, "I will go with you to the Embassy," thinking that I would not be granted the visa.

We went to the embassy at 3 a.m. to be the first in line. The unexpected happened. I passed all of the interview questions and received the visa. My father couldn't believe it. "God meant it to be, and there are lots of unknowns ahead of us," I told him.

Chapter 2

The preparations for traveling to the United State were not easy. I had saved only $3,000, but the cost of the trip was $1,000 and tuition was $2,400. When I went to submit my resignation to Kuwait National Industries, the general manager said, "The policy of the company states that you have to be employed for a year before you receive any vacation or benefit reimbursement; however, you have been a noble employee; therefore, I will issue a check for $1,000 as a gift for your service and when you graduate I want you to come back and work for us again."

I jumped up and down, kissed the man and said, "I will be back."

"Do you have a man like you that can take your job?" the manager asked.

"My brother Naji" I replied.

"Let him start working tomorrow," the manager said.

I was stunned that everything was going so smoothly.

Leaving my family behind in Kuwait was not easy for me. I knew that I had a major mission ahead of me. If I failed, the whole family failed. If I succeeded, the whole family succeeded.

I arrived in the United States on Aug. 18, 1980. For my first four months in the States, I had to attend the Intensive English Program at Pittsburg State University before enrolling in college classes. That was the easy step. The hard steps were dealing with being homesick, getting accustomed to the American culture, and discrimination against Arabs.

Nabil Seyam, Ph.D.

The first four months were very tough, as I was living independently for the first time and missing my family and friends. I called my family saying, "I want to come back home, I cannot live here, everything is strange." My father would say, "Coming back means failure, you must continue your mission."

The American culture was hard for me to accept. I had never seen a man and a woman kissing in public nor seen women wearing shorts. Being a religious person made it even harder. Eating at the university cafeteria at a specific time and food I was not used to was another issue I had to deal with. Staying with a roommate who was a stranger was another struggle. Seeing naked men in open showers was unbelievable, something you would never see in Muslim countries where Islam calls for modesty. My friends and I would wait until after midnight to take private showers in our shorts. For the first time, I was in a different world.

Around the time of my arrival in 1980, the crisis of the American hostages in Iran was the talk of the country. Surely, anyone who had dark hair must be an Iranian, many people thought. I witnessed my friends being beaten at gas stations. Many students were scared to go out after sunset. We were called sand niggers, flipped off, and treated badly.

After I paid the tuition, I had no money for other expenses. All of my Muslim friends would eat out every once in a while, but I did not have the money to go along. A friend directed me toward McDonald's, where I worked for just one week before I was fired. I've always had facial hair. The manager would always ask me to shave, which I usually did. The next day, he said, "Your beard is long, take this blade and go to the bathroom and shave." I said, "But I shaved this morning." He said, "I shave twice a day."

I went to the bathroom and shaved again to the point the blood was coming out of my face. The manager came in to the bathroom and witnessed the blood. He said, "Go home and never come back." At that time I decided to use my skills in martial arts and start teaching karate. I knew that financially I was a burden upon my family, but supporting myself for a short time worked very well. Still, I was aware of the reason I went to the States for — to study — and an outside job hindered that goal. Studying days and nights in a new language was interesting. I was able to finish two years of credit hours in only three semesters and a summer.

In the summer of 1982, I went back to visit my family in Kuwait. I was surprised to see that my family's economic situation had deteriorated. Although I was making a little income, still my family helped me pay the tuition. I was surprised to learn that my brother Naji was sending me all of his salary to support my education. "Since you left, we have not eaten fruits," my mother would say. My two-month vacation in Kuwait was a gloomy one.

After I arrived back in Wichita, I decided I wanted to marry and start a family of my own and to support myself instead of depending on my family back home.

In September 1982, I was introduced to Carrie through the girlfriend of a friend of mine. We got to know each other and learned that we both wanted to establish a family. Sixty-five days after our introduction, we were married. Carrie worked in the afternoon, and I went to school and later worked part time teaching karate and then worked at the university. By the end of 1984, we already had two kids, Melissa and Ahmad. Since we had little income I would take my daughter to school with me rather than paying a babysitter. Living in a one-bedroom apartment, watching David Letterman on a 13-inch black and white TV and driving a noisy 1974 Mazda were more than what we asked for. They were happy days.

In 1983, I started to have back pain that led to a slipped-disc operation. The limitations and pain even after the surgery did not stop me from continuing my education. I used to sit in the bathtub in hot water for hours just to be able to study. The pain was intolerable, but I had to graduate to fulfill my dream. For an entire year I would walk to the university crouching.

I graduated from Wichita State University in 1985 in the field of industrial engineering. A major dream of my parents had been fulfilled.

Graduation picture

The choice of staying and living in America after graduation never occurred to me. Wichita did not provide me or my children the needed Islamic environment to survive the western culture. Wichita's Muslim community did not have a full-time Islamic school or enough social activities to make Muslims want to stay. I always hoped to raise my kids in a Muslim country or an Islamic environment. So Carrie and I decided to move to Kuwait and raise our kids there. My marriage to Carrie had made me eligible for American citizenship, and in May 1986 I became a U.S. citizen.

Chapter 3

My two kids, Carrie, and I moved to Kuwait looking for opportunity and to be close to my family. Living in the same apartment with my family was one of many strange customs Carrie had to face. We had no choice but to accept that fact until I found a job. We were 15 in a two-bedroom apartment.

As visitors to Kuwait, we were told that we could not stay in the country more than 90 days if I didn't have a job. I applied for jobs all over the country, riding buses back and forth. After months of daily struggle in the hot weather of Kuwait, waiting at bus stops and traveling from city to city, I finally found work as a safety supervisor at Kuwait Entertainment City, an amusement park. Obtaining a job automatically granted me the right to change my legal status and obtain a work visa; however, my wife and kids were not guaranteed visas.

While I was asleep one afternoon, a knock came at the door of my family's apartment. A big, tall, strange Kuwaiti asked for me by name. My mother woke me up saying, "A Kuwaiti man wants you outside."

"Nabil Seyam, you are wanted by the Immigration Department of Kuwait, and I am here to arrest you," the man said. I understood that they were actually after Carrie and the kids. He pulled out a pair of handcuffs out and said, "Give me your hands." I said, "Please do not humiliate me in front of the crowds outside, I am not going to escape." He said, "You have the features of an honest man. Okay, I will not handcuff you."

While driving me in a government jeep, he turned the radio to FM rock music. "I love this music, this is the music you listen to right?" he said.

"I do not listen to rock music," I replied, surprising him with my feeling about the music, which is disliked under Islamic teachings.

At the immigration department I was told that I had to come up with a bond for myself and that I had 48 hours to come up with three tickets out the country for Carrie and the kids. If I did not come up with the tickets, I would be jailed. Knowing that I had not started working yet, nor had any income, I was forced to borrow money from friends. Carrie and the kids were deported 48 hours later to the United States, where they returned to Carrie's hometown of Wichita.

The departure of Carrie and the kids was a moment I will never forget. Seeing my wife and kids kicked out of a Muslim country because the visiting visa had expired! I felt like I had been stabbed in the back. At that moment, I realized how hard, complicated, and inhuman the laws of Kuwait were. I remembered that my brother, as a foreigner in Kuwait, was unable to get a driver's license for over 10 years, and how big of a difference there was between a Kuwaiti's lifestyle and a foreigner's. I realized how Kuwaitis treated their Indian or Filipino maids: like slaves, like animals. Despite all that, I deeply valued my family and my Kuwaiti home and had to accept the challenge and do my best to bring Carrie and the kids back no matter what it took.

For over a year and a half I was unable to bring Carrie and the kids back. The government would tell me that "you don't make enough money to raise a family here!" Although I was making a very good income, this and other rules were made up to make life hard on foreigners and to make it difficult to bring families to Kuwait.

During a conversation with a good Kuwaiti man, he stated, "It takes only one paper that states you have a high salary to be able to bring your wife." He was suggesting a way around the system, a scam, that worked like this: I would quit my current job and work without pay for a company that would say, on paper, that I was being paid a salary high enough to bring Carrie and the kids back.

During that time, Kuwait was witnessing a lot of explosions and terrorist attacks. Finding a job was almost impossible. Still, I had to take a chance so I could bring Carrie and the kids back.

I submitted my resignation and accepted an unpaid job with a company just to be able to bring my family back. My father thought I was crazy. "How could you resign and work for free, knowing that you will never find a good job like the one you had?" "God is the provider, not the people," I would say. Later I found out that it was not just a matter of filing a little paperwork with the government, that it was little more complicated. Eventually, after visiting a number of of government agencies and filing a lot of paperwork, Carrie and the kids were allowed back. Seeing Carrie and the kids again was another unforgettable moment of my life. Another mission accomplished.

While in Kuwait, Carrie went to work for an American school. I was blessed with a better job, working for Kuwait Metal Pipe Industries as a safety engineer, and the kids attended a private school. We were able to stand on our feet and have a very comfortable life. Carrie became pregnant with our third child, Yusef, who was supposed to be born in Kuwait. The pregnant Carrie and the kids went to the States to visit her family for the summer.

With fire brigade in Kuwait

Chapter 4

On Aug. 2, 1990, Saddam Hussein invaded Kuwait. Prior to the invasion, there were a lot of verbal accusations from the Iraqi regime, accusing Kuwait of stealing Iraqi oil. Some Arab leaders tried to defuse the conflict but had no luck. When Saddam Hussein presented the problem to the American ambassador, April Gillespie, in Baghdad, she stated that the conflict was between Iraq and Kuwait and the United States had no place in the conflict. These comments and these words were the green light for Saddam to invade Kuwait.

On Wednesday, Aug. 1, 1990, we had been watching TV, curious about what an Iraqi official had told the Kuwaiti crown prince: "You will not sleep in your home tonight." With these words I went to sleep not even thinking of what might be next.

As I was heading to work at 5:30 in the morning, listening to a recitation of the Holy Qur'an from the Kuwait radio station; a voice of a man through the microphone said, "O' Arabs, O' Muslims, Kuwait has been invaded by Iraq." My first reaction was disbelief, thinking someone was joking. As I got closer to work, which was about 60 miles north of Kuwait City, I started to hear what sounded like bombing. At that moment I realized that, Kuwait truly had been invaded.

Since I was the safety engineer of the company, I continued the trip to ensure that the emergency evacuation plan was executed. When I arrived, a meeting was held with a few of the engineers. At the company on Thursdays, all managers were off duty, and just the operations were working. When I arrived, I noticed that employees were being dropped off by company buses and the buses were leaving instead of staying as they usually did. That meant the workers had no transportation back home, a serious issue. The company is in an industrial zone away from any other transportation. We decided to evacuate all employees, and, since many engineers had cars, we agreed to transport as many employees as possible in our own cars. The plan worked. I was the last employee to leave the company. I closed the gate and headed south toward my family's apartment.

As I was driving on the highway, I noticed people driving the opposite direction. I did not know what was ahead of me as I headed toward my family's apartment.

My father had gone to work early not knowing that Kuwait had been invaded. What surprised us as residents of Kuwait was that the whole country was invaded by an outsider while people slept unaware. The Kuwaiti rulers and their families fled south to Saudi Arabia, escaping with their lives but not informing residents about the Iraqi forces approaching Kuwait.

That was a major issue for us to swallow: Who told the rulers of the Iraqi movement, and why weren't the people informed?

Within a few hours of the invasion, an Iraqi helicopter with an Iraqi flag flew over declaring the fall of Kuwait. Moments later we started to hear loud bombing not too far away. We later discovered it was the Crown Prince's Palace being bombed, an attack that lasted a whole day.

Thursday, the first day of the invasion, was very dangerous, and many families decided to stay home. On the second day of the invasion, I decided to drive and tour the country. My mother was shouting, "Are you crazy, where are you going?"

I was determined to witness the invasion and the Iraqi army in action. I drove north, east to Kuwait City, south and then west. Roads were almost empty of drivers, and many cars were abandoned. On the streets outside the Kuwaiti National Guard building, I saw many uniforms belonging to Kuwaiti troops who had shed them to avoid detection by Iraqis. I saw dead bodies. I saw the destruction of the Crown Prince's Palace. I saw the checkpoints that Iraqis had started to set up. I saw a gunfight between Iraqi forces and Kuwaitis who were shooting from an apartment building balcony. After more than three hours of driving, I couldn't wait to go back home to tell my family what I had seen.

After the Friday prayer, I was able to convince my mother — like me, she's curious and a risk taker — to come with me and witness the destruction. I drove all over the country, saw looting everywhere, and saw the army removing car motors and electric poles of the street. I saw computers and lab equipment being taken from the University of Kuwait and watched big trucks loading just about anything they could and move it north to Iraq. It was a scene of what I call "emptying Kuwait." That day I realized that Saddam's claim that Kuwait was part of Iraq was a false claim. Saddam had no intention of staying in Kuwait. How could someone destroy a country, claim the land, and then stay in it? Saddam wanted to ruin Kuwait but not stay in it. His hatred of the Kuwaiti and Saudi ruling families, along with the green light from the U.S. ambassador, had driven him to make the move.

On Saturday, the third day after the invasion, I went to work to see the condition of the company. I was very surprised to see the factory surrounded by Iraqi forces. Kuwait Metal Pipe Industries became an Iraqi company. I went in and found three other men surrounded by high Iraqi government officials negotiating how to transport all machines and production lines to Iraq. I demanded a meeting with the officials to negotiate a deal. The team and I were able to convince the Iraqi officials not to move the factory, but the tradeoff was that we agreed to return to work and produce oil and water pipes. We succeeded in delaying production for a few weeks until the high Iraqi officials left Kuwait. The trip to the company for the first week was just for the purpose of keeping it intact and to protect it from the Iraqi Government.

The increase in Iraqi checkpoints had reduced my movements to all but urgent missions. A friend who was a professor at Kuwait University asked me to join him on a trip to Kuwait University. As we were driving on the campus, we noticed a large gathering of Iraqi soldiers, with some of their comrades lined up for execution. We stopped the car and approached the big leader of the group and asked what was going on. The Iraqi leader said, "These soldiers are thieves. They stole food at night from the grocery store of the university, and they should be killed." We couldn't believe the situation: The whole country had been invaded and the Iraqi leader wanted to kill his soldiers because they stole food at night!

We were begging the leader of the group to let them go or give them another chance. After more than 20 minutes of pleading, he said, "Just for you, I'll set them free."

Day after day, the checkpoints were becoming more and more dangerous, as they had become targets of the Iraqi resistance.

Because I looked like an Arab, spoke the language, was polite, and provided Iraqi soldiers with water, I was able to pass many checkpoints easily.

The situation became worse by the day, and could not be described as anything but deteriorating. Banks had been closed for days after the invasion. One day, after more than five hours of standing in line at the bank, I was able to withdraw my savings. Later I discovered that all of the money that was given to us was unofficial currency that could not be used in the country. I still have the money until today.

Food was in short supply, and none of my family members had any source of income. During the invasion, I went to check on a friend who is Kuwaiti. I was shocked to learn that Kuwaitis were receiving food and other aid from known Kuwaiti organizations, but that only Kuwaitis were eligible. Even during the invasion of their country, Kuwaitis still received special treatment.

Because I was the only member of my entire family with a car, I was burdened with undertaking risky travel to bring food to my family. But it was not only my family, but many of our neighbors who had asked me for help.

After the Friday prayer, I noticed some families were selling food and making a good profit. They would travel to Basra, Iraq, two hours away, buying and selling goods. I knew that being an American citizen and driving in Kuwait was risky, but traveling all the way to Iraq was not just risky mission, it was stupid and crazy. But our condition pushed me to choose between either dying like an animal or dying like a hero for a good cause. As cover, I convinced my mother to travel with me to Iraq. In Kuwait I bought Pepsi, a used television and a VCR, a carpet, and other goods to sell in Iraq. We put most of the stuff on top of my Mazda station wagon and off we went.

Since Saddam claimed that Kuwait is part of Iraq, no borders existed, which made travel easier. The two-hour journey between Kuwait and Iraq was full of sadness. We saw Iraqi men walking all the way from Iraq into Kuwait "forced" to fight in the Gulf War. Many unarmed soldiers were walking in the middle of Kuwait's 120-plus-degree summer, barefooted without food or drink. We saw many army vehicles abandoned on the side of the road. As we approached Basra, we were stopped by an Iraqi military truck full of soldiers who surrounded the car with the intention of ambushing us. My mother screamed in their faces, "What do you need? Don't you fear God?" Suddenly, all of them backed off.

One sure way of knowing you are in Iraq is that Saddam's statues and huge pictures are all over the country. Such pictures and

statues of Arab leaders are put up by the people. It was forced upon the people. If you travel anywhere in the Middle East, you would observe that strange habit. It's what I call the psychology of idolism, which means the leaders are saying: I am your deity, love me or hate me, but I am everywhere you go.

Saddam statue

We approached Basra in the afternoon, not knowing anyone or where or how to sell what we'd brought. We decided to travel into a neighborhood to find buyers. As we turned into the neighborhood, boys and girls were running behind us looked curious. We stopped near a house where three Iraqi ladies were outside talking. We introduced ourselves and within three minutes all but the TV was sold. A very generous Iraqi woman invited us to dinner in her house. My mother and I accepted the invitation. It was unbelievable that a woman with seven children was able in just a few minutes to bake fresh bread, fry fresh fish and make a meal large enough to feed 15 people. I was not surprised by the woman's invitation but by the level of trust she demonstrated by inviting two strangers from a country hers was supposedly at war with.

On our way out of Basra, I told my mother we had to sell the TV to make more money. I stopped in the middle of the highway between Basra and Kuwait pointing that I had a TV for sale. An Iraqi civilian approached and asked me to show him the TV. When I opened the trunk, I was shocked to see that the buttons of the TV had melted. After a few words of negotiations, the TV was sold. With the money we made, we bought lots of eggs at the border between Iraq and Kuwait to resell in Kuwait. My family and I were able to survive the hard days of the invasion through buying and selling.

During the invasion many Kuwaitis had fled Kuwait south toward Saudi Arabia. With most Kuwaitis gone, Palestinians and other minority communities were the only people remaining behind. Many other nations evacuated their people through ships or busses.

During the invasion, I contacted the American Embassy to inform them of my family's phone number. A few days later I received a phone call from the Embassy saying that the last flight was heading to the States and they encouraged me to leave. Since Carrie and the kids were visiting her family in Wichita, I had not much to fear except for the safety of my family in Kuwait. So I decided to stay. Iraqi officials had announced that foreigners would be killed if they didn't surrender. Well, that meant that being a Palestinian with documents stating I was an American citizen was not a good thing in occupied Kuwait.

A Lebanese neighbor of my mother asked if I could take her to the market. I knew the danger, but I did not hesitate to say yes. I believe everything is in God's will. On our way back, we were stopped at an Iraqi checkpoint. That was the first time that I was asked for the car title, which Iraqis had started asking for because so many cars were being stolen in Kuwait. I presented the title to the soldier. Our neighbor was scared to death, knowing that I was a U.S. citizen. The soldier looked at my title, which like all other government documents showed one's religion and nationality, and then said, "Are you a U.S. citizen?"

Without any feeling I said, "How can I be a U.S. citizen and be speaking to you in Arabic? What you are reading is the model of the car." I was driving a Mazda!

The Iraqi soldier said we could leave, and I watched his reaction in the rear-view mirror as we started from the checkpoint, to see if he knew I was trying to fool him. I feared he was about to shoot us with a rocket-propelled grenade, but the lie had worked: He believed the car was American, not me.

As soon as we arrived home, the neighbor told the family, "We lived another life; your son is a risk taker; don't let him drive again."

Dealing with the soldiers was a daily struggle of the invasion of Kuwait. About 1 a.m. one day, we heard a hard knocking at the door. My little brother opened the door to find a whole bunch of Iraqi soldiers surrounding my family's apartment. First, I thought they were looking for me, but I learned from an Iraqi lieutenant that he was looking for my brother-in-law, a Kuwaiti citizen. As I was talking to the lieutenant, I recognized another man in the group that I knew from high school. He was a Palestinian who knew that my brother-in-law was a Kuwaiti citizen, but he claimed that my brother-in-law was with the Kuwaiti army. I said to the Palestinian man, "I know you and I am sure you recognized me, too. I can prove to you that my brother-in-law is not with the army nor he is with the Kuwaiti resistance."

While I was talking to the man, my other sister had already called my brother-in-law and told him the Iraqi army was looking for him. His immediate reaction was to leave the apartment and head to his family for refuge. I was able to convince the man that I would bring documents from my sister's apartment proving that my brother-in-law was not a soldier. The next day I delivered the documents, helping save my brother-in-law's life and keeping my entire family from being dragged into the struggle.

Iraqi soldiers started searching houses and apartments looking for Kuwaiti resistance and U.S. citizens. A month before the invasion, my apartment had flooded with sewage, which forced me to leave it. I rented a new apartment on the fifth floor, bought new furniture and fixed the apartment waiting for Carrie and the kids to arrive in mid-August.

I was living with my parents but used to visit the new apartment daily to be sure that everything is intact. The most scary incident I had is the day when my brother-in-law called me saying that the Iraqi army was in their neighborhood and that if they found his brother's army uniform they would kill the entire family. "Can you get rid of the uniforms?" he asked.

"This is a very dangerous mission, there are many Iraqi check-points, and I have to drive all the way to your neighborhood," I said.

"Please do it for me or we may all die," he replied.

As I was on my way with my mother, I noticed an excessive number of checkpoints on the way. After we arrived, immediately we put all the Kuwaiti army uniforms in the trunk. As we were heading back to my apartment so we could hide the uniforms, I noticed a long line of cars for detailed checking inside and outside of each car. My mother got scared and said, "That's it, we are dead."

Truly, I was speechless knowing our destiny, but I did not want to scare my mother more. As we got closer, I started to recite verses from the Holy Qur'an and asking God to protect us. As it was my turn in line, I said with confidence, "Hello, peace be upon you, may Allah bless you sir." He said, "Do you have guns?" I said, "No, let me open the trunk for you." Instead, he said "move quickly," telling us to go on. It was unbelievable that every car was searched but ours. It was another life. We drove slowly with strange feeling, and told my mother, "We had good intentions and God saved us. Did I not say everything is in his hand?"

As we were unloading the bags containing the uniforms, neighbors were watching us. Some of the women approached us with fear thinking I was with the resistance or even with the Iraqi army. After a few words of assurance, we convinced the neighbors that we were just trying to stash the uniforms.

Two days later, the security guard of the apartment building called to tell my family that the Iraqi army was in the neighborhood. My mother and I drove to the apartment before the Iraqi soldiers came in. We removed all the uniforms and threw them in the trash dumpster and burned them. Before we left the apartment I had a feeling that something was about to happen. I told my mother, "Let's write on the wall of the apartment 'Victory to Iraq.' This way the soldiers will believe we are with them so they will not destroy the apartment."

Within 45 days of the invasion, Kuwait became like an empty house. You would hardly see people driving anymore. Most if not all foreigners and Kuwaitis had fled the country. Due to the growing Kuwaiti resistance, any moving vehicle was a target by Iraqi forces. In every street and every corner we started to see more Iraqi armored vehicles being bombed. I escaped without harm an explosion of an Iraqi military truck that blew up only 20 feet from my passing car. I saw the truck go up in the air few feet. It was an unbelievable show. Within minutes, the truck became a piece of folded steel.

Witnessing the invasion of Kuwait, explosions, people disappearing, and the daily ambushing had led me to take a very risky step: Taking pictures of the destruction of Kuwait.

To keep Iraqi forces unaware of my mission, I took only a few pictures. The undertaking was riskier than I anticipated.

One unforgettable scene I witnessed was the scene of hanging of two Iraqi men accused of stealing food. They were hung on a crane in the middle of Kuwait City and left there for 15 days as a warning to others.

Tank in Kuwait

Broken Iraqi Truck

Fires in Kuwait

Fires in Kuwait

Iraqi tank in Kuwait

Battle from a building

Iraqi truck full of Kuwaiti stolen goods

Iraqi tank in Kuwait

Steeling cars using cranes

Battle from a building

A stolen door of a car

Iraqi tank in Kuwait

Battle at the Kuwaiti national guard

Battle at the national guard

On Oct. 1, 1990, at around 9 p.m., a Kuwaiti friend called asking for help. My brother and I went to his house knowing that we had to return before the 10 p.m. curfew. As we were leaving my friend's house, we were stopped at an Iraqi checkpoint. The street was well-illuminated, so I could see it was more than the usual checkpoint. A tall, slim Iraqi lieutenant stopped us and asked to see my driver's license, car title, and my brother's I.D. Knowing that this was an educated man and not a regular soldier, I knew my identity would be recognized. All I recall was a shout, "Get him, he is an American." Out of nowhere the soldiers approached my car pointing machine guns at us. I was dragged from the car and thrown to the ground. Fifteen to 20 soldiers pointed their guns at us. The scene is unforgettable; I can clearly see it now.

The lieutenant ordered one of his men to take my car away, telling me that "this car and all of your items belong to the Iraqi government. Give me your address." The Iraqi soldier drove my car over a one-foot concrete street divider and I recall thinking that — and it still strikes me as strange that I could think this under gunpoint — "My car. My car. He's wrecking my car."

Fortunately, my brother was able to present documents that he is an Arab, so he was let go.

While on the ground, I was pushed, pulled, and handcuffed extremely tightly, then dragged into an office that looked like a mobile home. Inside, I was tortured and interrogated for about two hours. "Why did you become a U.S. citizen? What are you doing in Kuwait? Are you a spy? Are you with the Israeli government? Are you with the CIA? You are a traitor. I fought for your country Palestine and you had become an American! You are a dead traitor. I am going to kill you." And on the interrogation went.

The lieutenant put his pistol on the table trying to scare me saying, "Renounce your U.S. citizenship and we'll set you free. Otherwise you are dead."

My refusal made him angrier, and he shouted and screamed bad language while I waited for him to pull the trigger. "We are introducing men like you on Iraq television, telling the world about how bad America is and how good the Iraqi government is. If you agree to do that, we'll set you free," the lieutenant said.

My continued refusal made him like a wild animal. At that moment, I saw death in my own eyes. The entire two hours of interrogation occurred while I was handcuffed, my hands tied with a wire rope behind my back and my head pushed against a window air conditioner, where my body shook with coldness to the point my toes were frozen, too. As I tried to answer his questions, he would cut me off and call me bad names.

Before I was captured, I had to use the bathroom so bad, but I told my brother I'd use it when I arrived at home. The cold freezing air coming out of the air conditioner made the situation worse. I was about to urinate all over the place, but I was thinking if I did so, the lieutenant would think I urinated due to his fear. I tried my best to hold it, but the pain was increasing. As of a result of that night, I still suffer tremendous pain above the groin area and have severe headaches. The lieutenant's attitude and behavior confirmed a belief in my heart that I would not come out of that night alive.

Looking back I can see that the mobile home was of a regular size, with only one room, a chair, a sofa, and a desk. Pistol and machine gun ammunition were all over the desk.

Suddenly two Iraqi intelligence officers with pistols on their sides came in to take me to unidentified area. While I was still handcuffed for more than two hours, they pulled me by my shirt out of the mobile home toward a car and drove me in the middle of the night. In the car both did not say a word to me. Observing where we were going, and knowing Kuwait very well, I noticed that I was taken to the SAAS hotel near the Persian Gulf. In the hotel, they freed my hands and I was assigned to a room. "Do not leave your room, we'll come and get you in the morning," one intelligence officers said.

While in the room I couldn't sit or stand, I had pain in my back, hands, stomach, and head. After using the bathroom right away, I opened the curtains to find that the room was actually on the shore of the gulf and surrounded by many soldiers. I did think of escape, but realized there was no way out. Knowing that the phone might be tapped or that I was being watched, I was careful when I called the U.S. Embassy and my family. At that moment I didn't care anymore. I was already tired, hungry, and in a bad condition.

Not knowing if I had really slept or not, I suddenly heard a pounding at the door and a man saying, "Come out." I was directed by an intelligence officer to head into a big hall where I noticed at least 25 hostages, mostly British. After we ate breakfast, we were told that we would be transferred to Baghdad. There was panic among the group, with many fearing they would die. Among the hostages was a pregnant British woman who was due at any moment. She was in a lot of pain, so she was left behind. My parents and my brother came to say goodbye, knowing it might be the last time they would see me alive. My father and mother were angrily telling the Iraqi: "He is an Arab like you despite his citizenship. Why are you taking him to Baghdad?" They said, "We follow orders." My parents were begging the Iraqi officials for more than 15 minutes without results. I sat in the long bus not knowing our fate. I looked at my parents crying.

As we were going through Kuwait, I was looking at empty streets and the destruction left behind. We were surrounded by Iraqi armed forces who led us all the way to Iraq. Because the journey was long, the other hostages and I had the chance to talk.

Being a dark-complexioned Arab-American might not be a good thing with a group of white Europeans and American hostages. Anyone in their place would think I was an Iraqi spy. As we were talking on the way, I said to them: "The Iraqi regime does not differentiate between an Arab-American, white American, or European. We are all considered foreigners, and we are wanted by the Iraqi regime."

The Iraqi soldiers in the bus were irritated because they couldn't understand our language, so I was forced to translate some of the conversations. One hostage cussed an Iraqi intelligence officer on the bus, and when I was asked for interpretation, I said, "He is saying hello."

Halfway to Baghdad, the driver stopped at a restaurant so we could have a meal. At the restaurant, we were guarded by many soldiers. All hostages but me ordered alcohol. Jokingly, one of the British hostages said, "There is no God in Iraq, there is only Saddam, so, drink Nabil." I said, "It is against my religion I cannot drink" because it is against my religion.

An hour later, the Iraqi officials ordered us to get in the bus. On our way, halfway between Basra and Baghdad, I noticed a brewery. I said to myself, "How could such a leader claim being a Muslim, and he allows a beer factory in his country?" It was obvious to me that Saddam's application of Islam was different than ours.

We arrived at Baghdad's Melia Mansour Hotel late at night after a long and exhausting trip. We were divided into two groups. The officials in Baghdad did not realize that I understood what they were saying, so I was able to understand and take advantage of the Arabic language. The officials told us, "We are keeping in the hotel those who are either old or sick, and others will be distributed throughout Iraq." The tall hotel was one of the targets in Iraq. It was like a headquarters, so if the hotel was to be hit, the hostages "guests of Iraq" would be hit, too.

Although I'd had the slipped-disc operation in 1984, I still had chronic back pain. I told the Iraqi, in Arabic, "I am very sick and I have to have back surgery soon. I have to be under medication." The Iraqi officials decided to keep me in the hotel, where we stayed on the ninth floor and ate at a restaurant on the top floor of the building. We were called "the guests of Iraq" by Saddam. Yes, we surely ate the best food and some of us slept in a five-star hotel, but it was a phony joke: We were human shields.

The first night defied reality: We were in Baghdad, not Kuwait any more. We were under the control of the Iraqi government. We were hostages.

After being placed in rooms, we were ordered to close the doors and not come out until morning. I was walking around the room looking for cameras and audio devices but found nothing. I still did not trust them; I knew we were bugged and watched. I made my prayers before I got on the bed and asked God to release me from this calamity. Again, the night passed so fast and all that I can recall is walking up holding my head due to a severe headache.

In the morning we were ordered to go up on the top floor to eat breakfast with other hostages. It was an open buffet type, and, I have to be honest, the food was good. On that same day, an American diplomat visited me and other American hostages. I was unable to say anything about the captivity or the torture, believing the place was bugged. "Don't drink Iraqi water; it is filthy," the U.S. diplomat said. He would visit us once or twice a day, bringing water and other necessary items.

In my group there were Americans, French, British, and Japanese. Watching them and their features, it was clear many hostages were in a very bad mood. Daily, the French and British diplomats would bring whiskey to the hostages. Many of the hostages would spend their days and nights drinking to avoid thinking of their fate. Most if not all of the hostages had given up on life. They either believed they would be killed or would die in Baghdad. A couple of British and French hostages were very sick, and one refused to eat or cooperate with the Iraqi officials. He had decided to isolate himself from the group.

Iraqi government officials used to bring an Iraqi doctor to check on our conditions daily. I was taking Ibuprofen and Tylenol many times a day.

I became very close to the hostages and was aware of their feelings; I started to treat them as my own brothers, sons, or father. I would deliver food personally to the sick ones, whom the Iraqis thought were carrying infectious diseases but were actually either sick from the stress or conditions like high blood pressure. Seeing the hostages' conditions deteriorate made me feel bad that there was nothing I could do. They were innocent people, and I cared so much for them.

We were allowed two hours each day to walk in the hotel campus. Soldiers were all over the place, on top of the hotel, on the sides, on

41

the roads, and sitting around us. All of them carried machine guns or pistols. Escape wasn't possible.

I was under a lot of stress thinking of my family in Kuwait and Carrie and the kids in the States. I knew that Carrie was due with our third child around Oct. 1, the day I was taken hostage. I knew that she should have had the baby by now, but I had no news from anyone and was unable to contact anyone outside the hotel. As I was walking in the lobby of the hotel guarded by Iraqi soldiers, I noticed a gymnasium-like hall. I asked the soldier if I could train inside. Since I have a first-degree black belt in karate, I thought I could stretch and make some moves that might help reduce my back pain. Within 15 minutes, an Iraqi karate expert was brought up to the gym to show his strength. I knew that was a hint to not try to start anything.

Nabil Seyam with a French hostage

Being in the room by myself for a long time was so boring. When the diplomat came, I asked if he could find me a small radio to hear the news. By that night, I had a nice transistor radio. I was so excited to hear the news and what I had missed in the past days. The Iraqi did not find out about the radio.

Chapter 5

The other hostages and I started to develop a close relationship with an Iraqi waitress at the hotel restaurant who was very nice and felt sorry for us. One day, I took advantage of her niceness and asked if she could call my family in Kuwait. Initially she refused, knowing that she might be killed. I begged her, saying: "You are doing me and my entire family a Godly favor. No one will know about it, trust me please." A few days later she agreed. Within 24 hours, my mother, father, and brother arrived at the Melia Mansour Hotel. My family had ridden a bus from Kuwait to Baghdad, a 12-hour trip through hundreds of checkpoints, just to see me.

At the hotel they asked for me but were told that, surely, no one here knows anything about any hostages! My family stayed in another hotel that night, and in the morning they contacted the Jordanian and Palestinian embassies trying to locate me. That was the first time both embassy officials knew about an Arab-American hostage in Baghdad. Both embassy officials told my family, "It would be better to communicate with the American Embassy. Your son is a U.S. citizen, and there is nothing we can do." They headed right over to the U.S. Embassy.

The U.S. Embassy did more than help; they brought my family to the hotel. It had been more than 12 days since we had seen one another. Our first meeting was really emotional. I asked my family if they have heard anything about Carrie and the kids. They said, "No, calls to the U.S. were disconnected."

Parents and brother in Baghdad

I asked them to bring toothpaste, a toothbrush, and some underwear, since I had worn the same clothes for nearly 10 days. Within that same week, many reporters visited the hotel, publicizing our condition. While I was waiting for my family to come back again, I was introduced to a Palestinian journalist who was a representative of the Jordanian ministry of information. The Melia Mansour Hotel was in the spotlight as the world media followed our stories. I told the Palestinian journalist of my situation, that I was forced to come to Baghdad, that my only crime was being a U.S. citizen. For him and other media personnel, finding an Arab-American hostage was unusual. I had interviews with many international news agencies.

My family decided to visit the Jordanian and Palestinian embassies once again, but they were turned away. In fact they were told, "The only one who can release your son is Saddam." My family left very upset, as they knew they would get no help from Saddam.

The United States, Britain, France, Japan and other governments were sending representatives and famous people to obtain the release of as many hostages as possible. Jesse Jackson, a former British top government official and others tried to visit Saddam. I met singer Cat Stevens, who had taken the name Yusuf Islam after adopting the Muslim faith, at the Melia Mansour Hotel as he was trying to meet with Saddam to release some British hostages. I explained to him my situation, and that I had a family in Kuwait and in the States that needed me. He promised he would do his best to help.

A Palestinian journalist promised that he would contact the Iraqi Ministry of External Affairs to discuss my condition. He also told me, "I will personally contact his Majesty King Hussein (of Jordan) and explain your condition. Having a Palestinian hostage in Iraq is not acceptable." The journalist disappeared for couple of days. I thought at first that he was full of it.

The fifteenth day of being a hostage was a turning point. The journalist contacted my family in Kuwait and assured them that I would be released soon. "You are imprisoning an Arab in your country," the Palestinian journalist said he told the Iraqi external ministry officials. "You either release him or the lead news will be an Arab hostage in Iraqi hands," A few minutes later the journalist received the news: I would be freed. The day was Oct. 16.

On that same day, my parents traveled again to Baghdad, bringing clothes and other items. Immediately after my release, the American diplomat took me in a diplomatic car away from the hotel to the U.S. Embassy. Carrie and I had not spoken since the invasion. I was very curious to know if she had a boy or a girl and how she and the kids were doing.

"I had a boy and called him Yusef, after the prophet 'Joseph.' Peace be upon him," Carrie said. I was very happy and relieved to

45

hear that she and the kids were doing well and that she had named our son Yusef. Yusef the prophet faced a lot of struggle in life and he also was put in prison. Carrie had Yusef on the same day I was taken hostage, at 9:01 p.m. Central Time, at the same exact time I was taken hostage in Kuwait.

Our conversation was not long, but she asked when I was coming back. I was confused and did not know which direction to go: Back to Kuwait, where my family was? Or to the States where Carrie and the kids were? I told Carrie, "I don't like staying with anyone, and I don't have money to support the kids now. Therefore, I have to think of how to tackle this issue."

The American diplomat informed me that Kuwait was a dangerous place, and there was no way they would allow me back there. "We will fly you out of here," the diplomat said.

"I want to take you in a tour around Baghdad before you leave the country," the diplomat said. We drove close to Saddam's palace and visited other important sites. I was shocked to see the thousands of helmets molded in one of the famous streets of Baghdad, and asked the diplomat why they were there. "These are the helmets of some Iranian soldiers who were killed during the Iraqi/Iranian war," he said. I couldn't believe it, saying, "Is Saddam proud of his achievement — killing Muslims?" The diplomat replied, "He must be!"

The American diplomat informed me that CNN, ABC, NBC, CBS and other news agencies would like to interview me. "Be sure not to say anything that would jeopardize your life," the diplomat said. "Don't worry," I said, "I'll be calm." The diplomat and I went to the U.S. ambassador's house in Baghdad. There I was introduced to about 20 Americans who had taken refuge in the house. The back yard was full of reporters. During interviews, I recall saying, "Kuwait is like an empty house; we lost everything." Afterward, we ate a meal with the rest of the Americans.

World news

Later in the day, the diplomat drove me to a hotel where my family and the Palestinian journalist awaited me. There we ate our last meal in Iraq. While we were eating, I was distressed to see Muslims drinking alcohol, something I had never seen in Kuwait. The next morning, I visited with my family for a short time and I assured them I would bring the entire family to America to live together again, a promise I was eventually able to fulfill.

Around 9 o'clock, the diplomat and I headed to the airport for my departure from Iraq. The airport officer looked thoroughly through my luggage, asking if I had any money, cigarettes or other contraband, to which I said no. As I was walking in the terminal, I kept feeling like someone was about to call my name. I did not believe that I was out of Iraq until the plane took off. At that moment I said, "Al hamdu Lilah — Thank God."

A few minutes later we landed in Amman, Jordan. At the airport I was told that I had to go into Amman and head to the embassy to obtain a ticket to the States. A Jordanian immigration officer asked about my father's nationality, and I said he was Palestinian who held a Jordanian passport. "Well," he said, "before you leave Amman airport to the States, you have to bring us a release to leave the country."

"What do you mean, a release?" I said.

"You are considered a Jordanian citizen," he said, "and no Jordanian citizen can leave the country without permission."

I went crazy; I couldn't believe it! While a hostage, both the Jordanian and the Palestinian embassies rejected me, saying, "You are a U.S. citizen."

Knowing how complicated the rules are in the Middle East, I knew that I could be facing captivity again, this time in Jordan.

As I headed toward the luggage area, I was surprised to see dozens of reporters and cameramen. I was asked to tell what had happened in Kuwait. I couldn't hide the stress on my face and told the reporters of the emptying of Kuwait and other details of the invasion.

As soon as I was done, I took a taxi to the U.S. Embassy, where I was received with warmth and respect. Embassy officials handed me the ticket for a 10:30 flight that evening. While at the embassy, thinking of how to leave Jordan peacefully, I felt an angel from above tell me, "Contact your grandmother in Amman. She has the solutions." I hadn't seen my Lebanese grandmother for over 20 years and didn't know where she lived or how to contact her. I asked the U.S. diplomat if I could call my family in Kuwait and get my grandmother's phone number. I called my grandmother and said, "I am in Amman and I need to see you."

She gave me her address immediately and said, "I will be waiting for you outside." During the taxi ride, I sat quietly thinking of all the bad things I had faced and the difficult situation I would face at the airport that night. The minute we arrived at my grandmother's apartment, I recognized her easily, as she had lost her arm in the civil war in Lebanon during the Israeli invasion. She cried like a baby saying, "You are the son of my daughter, Amienha." While we ate, she said, "You look thin and worried, what happened to you?" I told her the whole story, including what I would be facing at the airport. She said, "Don't worry, my husband, Abu-Ahmad, knows a lot of Jordanians who work at the airport, and they can help you out."

Within a few minutes, two men came in and said, "We have contacted our connection at the airport, and they assured that you will be taken care of."

"I need someone to come with me," I said. "I cannot afford one more day of struggle. At the airport they have no mercy." The men said they would go with me.

On the way to the airport, I recited verses from the Holy Qur'an and asked God for guidance. As I approached the immigration booth, my heart was beating rapidly. A man that I had not seen before approached the officer and whispered in his ear. The officer said, "Have a nice trip Nabil."

I said to myself, "It is amazing, people who have connections can get away with anything, and those who don't have connections must suffer."

As I was taking the stairs and not looking back, I sped up my steps to leave the immigration officials behind. I was saying to myself, as long as I am at the airport I am not going to feel relaxed, and leaving is the only cure for that feeling.

The destinations were Rome, New York, Chicago, and then Wichita. Everything went smoothly when we arrived in Rome, but by that time that I looked awful — unshaven, dirty black circles around my eyes, and very sleepy. When it was time to depart, I was the only non-Caucasian heading to America. I was asked to step aside. Four officers suddenly surrounded me and took me aside. "Are you an American? Is this your passport? What are you doing here? Where did you come from? Why you are going to America? Where is your luggage?"

I told them my story, but they did not believe it. They took me all the way to the airplane to pull my luggage. "Is this your luggage? Do you have any weapons? Prove that you are a U.S. citizen." I was lucky that my family had left some pictures of blonde Carrie and the kids. Still, they weren't convinced I was telling the truth.

"I can't believe it, guys. Do I need look like an American 'white' to be an American?" I was shouting. "I am sick and tired of this. In Kuwait, Iraqi rejected me as an Arab. In Iraq, the Jordanian and Palestinian embassies rejected me as a Jordanian or Palestinian. In Jordan, they treated me as a Jordanian, and now in Rome, you are treating me as an Arab, not as an American."

"All of you are hypocrites; all of you are cowards," I shouted.

After searching my luggage and ensuring I was not a threat, the officer said: "Let him go." The airplane was already delayed 20 minutes. As I got on the plane, the last one to board, everybody looked at me strangely. I understood their feelings. We were in the midst of a serious conflict in the Middle East and I did look like a terrorist — to them.

I sat in the middle seat heading to New York, saying to myself, "Finally, I will be home soon."

A man came up to me and said, "Are you Nabil Seyam?" I though to myself, "Here we go again, is he a CIA or what?", but replied that, yes, I was Nabil Seyam. "I would love to do an interview with you; I have heard about you, welcome home," the reporter said. Twenty minutes later, the pilot said over the intercom, "We are honored to have the freed American hostage Nabil Seyam with us tonight." Greeters started to come from all over the plane. It was an unforgettable trip.

I arrived in Wichita around 10:20 p.m. on Oct. 19,1990, greeted by Carrie, the kids, the newborn baby that I had not seen before and many friends. Reporters were all over the place and Wichita local news ran a live report of my arrival. For the next 24 months I was in the spotlight, lecturing, visiting schools, churches and colleges, talking about my experience and the invasion of Kuwait.

Seeing Carrie and the kids after four and a half months reminded me of the separation caused by the deportation of Carrie in the kids from Kuwait. It had been difficult, but we came to tell ourselves

Nabil Seyam, Ph.D.

that it had been our destiny to be apart for a period of time due to uncommon causes.

Chapter 6

W e stayed with Carrie's family for the next three months, with all of us sleeping on the basement floor. My first week was what I call recovery. I would get up in the middle of the night standing with a fist ready to fight. I had many nightmares. Dreams of dead bodies, the invasion, the checkpoints, and the humiliation flashed all over the night. Having a family to support, back pain, and no work all had increased my stress.

To support my family and the newborn baby, we had to apply for food stamps and government aid. I'll never forget the days as we would go shopping after midnight, feeling ashamed of using the food stamps.

Carrie's mother helped us through her employer by donating money and furniture. I applied for jobs all over town but had no success. I worked as a temporary employee for a short time, but due to my back pain I couldn't handle assembly work.

In February 1991, after four months of struggle, I finally found a job with the local government, as an engineering inspector. The nature of the job required site visitations and inspections. While observing construction projects, I would study for my master's degree in safety engineering. After I finished the master's degree, I decided to continue all the way and obtain a doctorate in safety engineering, which I received in 1998. It is hard for a Muslim with an Arabic name to compete with Caucasians. For us even before 9-11, it was hard to find a job in many fields. Many white people are preferred over us in industries. That's why many of us try to achieve the highest level of education in order to compete with whites who may have only bachelor's degree.

My back pain worsened during my employment with the local government, and it was recommended that I have my back fused. Even after the fusion, the pain never went away and, in fact, sometimes I think it is worse.

Everything started to look brighter and brighter. Carrie and I bought a house, and we were able to live a very comfortable life once again. We decided to have another child and by the blessing of God she had our beautiful daughter Anisa. My oldest kids, Melissa and Ahmad, were going to public schools, and my mother and father had moved to the States. All the signs of happiness were obvious.

After obtaining the Ph.D., I was ready to make a move, but the destiny of God was ahead of me. In the summer of 1998, I was interviewed by a Texas-based recruiter to work in Saudi Arabia as a safety engineer for a metal company. More than 50 people applied for the job from all over the world. After several interviews, I was chosen.

The Saudi-based company asked that I come for visa and other paperwork and to address legal issues. Knowing that I had the job, I resigned from my volunteer duty as the director of Annoor Islamic School, told Carrie to start packing and said let's get ready to move again.

The company has offered me an annual $75,000 tax-free salary, an annual trip to the States for the whole family, free schooling, a villa, car allowance, and more. The Saudi company officials put me up in a five-star hotel in Bahrain, near Saudi Arabia. In the morning we were ready to sign the contract and talk about the visa. The human resources manager asked where I was from originally. "Palestine," I said.

"Where is your grandfather from?" he asked. Again, I said "Palestine."

"Sit down, we need to talk," he said. "Usually when we don't have a qualified Saudi to fill the position, we request assistance from foreign countries. Since you are an Arab, we have to talk about another scale."

"What do you mean by scale?" I asked.

"We give Arabs less salary than what we give Americans or Europeans," the manager said.

"Why?" I said. "Did they come from Mars and we came from the desert?"

"That's our policy," he said.

And, I said to myself, "That's why most of educated Arabs and Muslims don't work in the Middle East, because the laws are backwards."

My last words to the manager were, "I have a dignity, and my dignity is worth more than what you and your company worth." I turned my back and headed out of the room. Immediately, I called the recruiter in Texas and informed them of the situation. Their reaction was, "We can't believe it!"

In February 1999, I was offered a great opportunity to work for a major company, York International, as manager of health and safety. I worked there for two and a half years, the best of my career. The people were great, I had the best boss ever, and the company was very supportive of me and my leadership. I have left many fingerprints there that would last forever.

While working at York, I was asked to teach night classes for the local branch of Pittsburg State University. Despite my busy schedule, I accepted that opportunity. I believed I was offering a noble service by sharing my expertise with the next generation.

In July 2001 while working at York, I received a phone call from York headquarters in Pennsylvania, asking if I would accept the position of director of safety and health for the whole company. That call was one of those that keep you silent for a moment. I asked for some time to think about this big move. I went home very excited but not knowing what decision to make. I wanted the position, but I needed my kids in an Islamic school and a Muslim community. York, Pennsylvania, did not offer that. The opportunity would come just once in a lifetime and wasn't one I thought I could turn down.

But what should I sacrifice? My career? My community? My kids' Islamic education and environment? I prayed to God and asked him to help me make the best decision that would not jeopardize our faith.

While I was lost in thought wondering what to do, knowing that I had to reply to the head office as soon as possible, I received a phone call from a recruiter out of the blue. "Dr. Seyam, there is an opening near you with a well-known international company. They are looking for a corporate director of health and safety, would you be interested in talking to me?" I said without feeling, "Oh my God, I can't believe it."

"Are you talking to me?" the man said.

"No," I replied and asked him to please call me at home that night to discuss the opportunity, which was at a company in Wichita.

After a few days of negotiation, I accepted an interview with the president, senior vice president of human resources, and others. Within a few days, I signed the contract to start on Sept. 20, 2001.

The terrorist attacks on America occurred on Sept. 11, 2001. At that time, I was still at York working out my last days after giving notice. I received a phone call from my current company's human resources representative asking if I was still going to join the company.

"Why should I change my mind?" I asked.

"Well, I thought what has happened in New York may have changed your decision to join us," the representative said.

"No, I have committed to your company," I said.

The first week with my current company was very strange. Here was a man who looked Middle Eastern, is Middle Eastern, and has a dark complexion, kinky hair, a beard and a moustache. And here he was walking the factory floor in front of Americans shocked by an evil act committed by people who looked like me. That feeling bothered me for a long time. During my first public meeting speaking before many employees, I noticed some guys covered their mouths, others smiled, and others just stared. I knew it was my accent and looks. I said to myself, this is me and this is the way I am and this is the way I look and their remarks should not affect me. With that attitude, I was able to pass that and many other tests.

In the safety and health field, I was well respected by many hourly employees. In a short time they found out that where I came from or what my faith was did not matter. They looked at me as a professional who cared about their safety. Once as I toured the factory, I noticed that someone had drawn a long beard over a picture of me to look like Osama Bin Laden. Initially, I felt bad, but later I decided it was a price we have to pay for the action of others and there was not much we could do.

graduation

Having a Ph.D. sometimes has disadvantages, depending on who you work for and the personality of your boss. If you work as a consultant or for a university, having a Ph.D. is essential. In industry, it is little different. At a former employer, my boss told me: "It does not make sense to have the title Ph.D. after your name, because it does not look good in our type of business." Another boss said, "Your certificates on the wall are intimidating." Again, these are the personalities we have to deal with in our daily struggles as educated Muslim Americans.

During the last four years of my marriage to Carrie, our relationship deteriorated. We would argue and fight a lot. In 1996 I suggested that we go to the holy city of Mecca to conduct the pilgrimage, the Hajj. One of my goals was for both of us to come home as new people, cleansed and ready to start a new life. Hajj was a unique experience. There you find millions of Muslims who have the same ideology, direction, faith, book, God, and prophet. Regardless of where they come from, all of them pray the same way. All of them look like one person. That is the only place where you see the unity of Islam and Muslims.

Although the Hajj was a moving and unique experience, our situation worsened by the day. I had prayed to God to help us with the marriage because I knew how bad divorce was. Having headaches, arguing in front of the kids, and talking to myself led to seriously thinking about terminating the relationship. We'd had 18 years together and to dissolve our marriage would be a shame. The issue was not who was right or who was wrong; the issue was things were not going in the right direction.

While at the mosque praying and asking God to help me making a wise decision, the answer came immediately. I decided to step on my heart and divorce Carrie. She had asked for divorce many times before, but I thought time might change our condition.

We sat in the basement talking peacefully about a peaceful divorce. After a few minutes of negotiation, we both agreed on a peaceful divorce and that we would not tell anyone about the divorce until it was final. At that moment, we both felt that was the end of our relationship. There was no turning back.

After 60 days, the divorce was announced. Although many couples divorce, ours was much gossiped about. Rumors and insults came from both men and women. I heard many stories that I couldn't believe would come out of a Muslim's mouth. Although divorce is lawful in Islam, I was looked at as if I would be the last who to divorce. Still, I survived the gossip and continued preaching, lecturing, and leading prayers. However, Carrie has chosen to seek friends outside the Muslim community.

Many divorcees speak ill of their ex-spouses, but I have not talked ill since the day of my divorce. Islam has always taught me to remember the good days you had with your spouse and that gossiping is a major sin.

Carrie and I have dedicated our lives to serve our kids. Since our divorce, the relationship has turned more into one of mutual respect for one another for the best of the whole family.

My lifestyle is not like that of many people. I work full time and have dedicated my personal time to serve my family and the community. On weekends, I speak all over the state of Kansas on politics, Islam, multicultural issues, and conflict resolution. After work, I am involved with other issues with the community; teaching at universities; and other responsibilities. So I need to have a wife to help support me and the needs of my children.

Within a few days of the divorce, I contacted my sisters in Kuwait and asked if they had an Arab friend who was interested in getting married and moving to the United States. "Definitely, we have many friends," my sisters said.

The Islamic and Arab culture is unique when it comes to getting married. First the man and his family investigate and acquire knowledge about the family and the woman they want to ask to marry. They ask about their daughter, mother, father, and even brothers and sisters. Families that are not respected or troubling are usually avoided. Well- respected men and women are highly sought after.

So I traveled to Kuwait seeking a wife. When I arrived, I told my sisters, "I have only 10 days to find a good woman." They said, "We have contacted 13 of our friends and that their families are expecting you." In four days we visited many families. Some we visited for only 15 minutes; some we would sit with for about 30 minutes. There is nothing in Islam that is called "arranged marriage"; the man and woman sit and talk. He and she ask one another as many questions as they need. Both families request information on each party. It is not buy or sell. It is a life commitment between a husband and wife. No woman can be forced to marry another man. Islamically, it is forbidden. In fact, in Islam, the woman sets the value of the dowry (a gift such as gold), and she has all the right to draft her marriage contract.

More than half of the women we met were not my type: educated, outgoing, having social graces but still down-to-earth. One of the families we met was Susan's, which was well respected and had all that I asked for. Both families had an interest in exploring the opportunity. Susan requested a private meeting with me to discuss many issues before she would say yes or no. Her family would investigate who Nabil Seyam was and what he did in America.

Susan and I met in a big living room and discussed issues while members of our families socialized. We talked for about four hours and found we share a lot of common ground, that we shared many of the same likes and dislikes, such as food, that we'd both been through the struggle of divorce. The family invited us back the following day to answer my request to take the hand of Susan.

In our previous private meeting, Susan and I agreed to be engaged and to see how things would go during a six-month engagement period. We spent the next four days touring Kuwait and visiting lots of sites in the company of her relatives. Under Islamic law, a man and a woman cannot be alone unless they are officially married.

A humble engagement party was conducted, with immediate relatives invited.

The six-month engagement was a long enough period to know one another and to see if we could move on to the next step: getting married. In the Western world, dating is essential prior to getting married. In many cases a boyfriend-girlfriend relationship starts with a hug, a kiss, sexual relations. It might involve a child, marriage or living together. In Islam, adultery and fornication are forbidden.

Many ask how are you going to know the person if you don't sleep with them? Our answer has always been, get engaged and do not break the laws of God and then get married if you believe this is your future spouse.

After six months of communication via telephone, letters, and e-mails, Susan and I decided to marry. I traveled once again to Kuwait and within 24 hours we were married.

Since my marriage to Susan, I have been blessed with a child and many other bounties. Many of my dreams have been fulfilled. My mother, father, and most of my brothers and sisters have moved to the States. I bought a house in an upscale neighborhood on a golf course. In addition to my current work as corporate director of health and safety for an international company, I have been teaching a safety engineering course at night as an adjunct instructor for Wichita State University.

Since I am a man who wears many hats and likes to try anything that would help spread the true face of Islam, I have hosted a series of ethnic shows on local public television called ZYGO. Hosting the show has helped inform the public of how diverse the world is and that although we all may have come from different places we have a lot of similarities.

My opinion and publicity in the state of Kansas has led the publisher of Q&A Times to ask me to participate as a writer in the Sedgwick County magazine, giving the Islamic perspective on issues affecting people's daily lives. This great opportunity has given me the chance to freely present Islam the way it should be presented.

To remind myself of how far I have come, I keep a 13-inch television on a shelf in my garage so that each morning as I get into my car I have to look at it. A dozen years ago, to ease the stress of those early days in Wichita, I watched "Late Night with David Letterman" on it. I never thought I'd buy a 60-inch TV.

David Letterman

This new life I am living is more than a success story. It is full of happiness regardless of the pain and suffering I have faced or am still facing. God meant it to be this way. I don't think about tomorrow anymore. I want to live each day as it comes. I want to do my best to utilize every second of the day in something productive. I always believed that, if yesterday is like today, you have accomplished nothing. I had many goals in my life; I have achieved most of them. My ultimate success will be reached when I see all of my six kids successful and happy.

To be happy, you have to struggle. Nothing is free; even smelling air is costly. I've learned to climb the ladder step by step. In America,

My son Ahmad delivering the graduation speech

you can be anything you want to be. Most foreigners have taken the advantage of all the comfort we have in the country and succeeded. Living in America and not utilizing the freedom, the assets, the lifestyle, the education, and the opportunities is a waste of time. If I can make it, anyone else can. You need to travel outside the United States to see how fortunate you are in America. Many countries don't even have available hot water. We eat meat or chicken every day. I know many people overseas who may eat meat or chicken once a month. Many of us sleep on waterbeds and fancy mattresses, but overseas many sleep on the floor. We are blessed in America, but the problem is not many appreciate the blessings of God. The only time many of us would appreciate these bounties is when we lose them.

Although I see myself as a successful man, life has taught me not to be too excited. Overnight I may lose everything. The bounties I have today are trials from God and they will be witness on me in the judgment day. We are living in an era full of surprises. We are living in an era full of lies and accusations. We are living a history full of what I call "eliminate who opposes you." After 9-11, life for successful Muslims in America is no longer fun.

Chapter 7

When I came back from Kuwait, I was very disappointed that the Wichita Muslim community had not moved forward. Although the community was growing, we did not have a full-time Islamic school, our local mosque was too small to accommodate all Muslims, and parking was a major problem.

I have always been active in the Wichita Muslim community, but in the 1980s I and others never thought of an Islamic school as a priority. Many of us, including myself, were busy building our own faith through praying and increasing our knowledge of the Islamic faith.

Unfortunately, many of the previous Muslim generations have become westernized, having taken up drinking, premarital sex, and other non-Islamic values. They may carry an Arab or a Muslim name, but they are western. Learning from that experience, today's Muslims are little bit smarter.

Many of the Muslims who came to America before the 1980s did not think seriously of establishing full-time Islamic schools. Instead, their first priority was establishing places of worship. The problem with that was that it took care of the needs of that generation but not of the ones that followed. Today, the Muslims of America are totally the opposite. Most believe we have to start an Islamic school, then a place of worship, noticing that many of our previous Muslim generations are not practicing Islam.

The Muslims of Wichita started Annoor Islamic School "Sunday school" in 1989. The school was moderate and did not fulfill the dreams of all parents. I joined the school's board of education in 1993. The situation of the part-time school and the communication style between board members and the teachers was of the old days. I and other new board members requested changes because we wanted the school to grow. I was the secretary of the board for a few months until the director of the part-time school accepted a job offer and moved to another state.

Becoming the director of Annoor Islamic School "part time" has given me the freedom to work independently to bring about my vision of the school.

Many Muslims are attached to a strict culture that is not even Islamic. Many Muslims carry habits that they have learned from parents; however, they are more harming than building. Unfortunately many Muslims are afraid of any changes, they may call them innovation. I and many struggle daily with many Muslims who carry nothing but culture, but they believe it is Islamic. For example, a Muslim man may walk by a Muslim woman and not say hi or even look at her face, but he would say hi, smile, and look at a non-Muslim woman. This is one of many examples that are purely culture but not necessarily Islamic. It is not easy to change people over night it takes a lot of effort and perseverance.

Under the new leadership, the Annoor Islamic School grew rapidly. We changed the curriculum, emphasizing Arabic language and Qur'anic recitation, and hired many new teachers. I spent many hours volunteering trying to attract as many families and students to the part-time school. I recall the number of students jumped in 1994 and 1995 from 23 to 125. In the summer of 1995, we had to rent a public school just to accommodate the students and their needs. Deep in my mind I already had a plan to establish a full-time Islamic school, but the timing was not yet right.

Despite of the success of the Sunday school, personally I was not satisfied deep inside. We had lost many students to public schools in their early times by not having a full-time Islamic school.

In public school, God does not exist, but condoms do. Manners and morals are not taught, but how to contact the SRS is. Students take their bodies there, but forget half of their brains and all of their spirit somewhere else. The first place kids are exposed to sex is in public schools. Public schools teach safe sex, but God teaches us that fornication and adultery is unlawful. The comparison is irrelevant.

Noticing what happened to our previous Muslim American generation placed heavy burden on me to establish a full-time Islamic school. The success of the part-time Islamic school and the reputation we earned were influential in attracting families to a full-time school.

In 1995, I was selected by the community to lead the part-time school for a second term as director. I promised the community that we would have a full-time Islamic school in 1996. The idea was accepted by the school board. Establishing a full-time Islamic school takes time and effort. For one entire year I would spend hours and hours typing policies, researching, consulting other Islamic and private schools, traveling to visit all different sorts of schools to gain as much knowledge as possible to run the school. The challenge became harder due to the fact that we were unable to find a building for the school. The community tried everything, from buying a school or a church to anything that could be utilized as a school.

Nabil Seyam, Ph.D.

Around March 1996 I started visiting churches in the area to see if they have a section of a building we could rent. I visited · hundred of churches in town but had no success. I contacted Inter-Faith Ministries and spoke to the director. He suggested a few other churches. "We would love to rent you our building," said the Rev. Dr. Robin McGonigle of Pine Valley Christian Church, but the church's board had to make a final decision.

I met with the board and told them of the nature of the school and convinced them how important it was to our community. The church's board was gracious and humble enough to accept us into their building. The relationship between the Muslims of Wichita and the Christians of the Pine Valley church strengthened. We had many social activities, potlucks, and religious gatherings.

I knew what some Muslims might think of having an Islamic school in a Christian church, but I was looking at the long-term goal: a full-time Islam school in our own building. I knew some members would reject the idea, but we had to start somewhere even if it was going to cause distress.

I decided to face the community to inform them of the idea of having an Islamic school in a church. When I met with the community at the old mosque in Wichita, some Muslims doubted my faith. "We'd rather have our kids in public school than in a church," some said. For a week, I received some bad phone calls from Muslims calling me Kafir ("unbeliever") and some would never say Salam ("peace/hi") when we meet. Others just gave me dirty looks. Knowing the culture, I knew what I was about to face and ready for it. I met the accusations with patience and humbleness. I was saying to some of them, "Tomorrow you will discover I am right."

All I needed was 12 committed families to start a preschool. By April, I was able to convince 12 Muslim families to send their kids to the new, full-time Islamic school at Pine Valley Christian Church. We signed a one-year lease with them and hired teachers. We started the school in August 1996. During the day, some curious Muslims would visit the school to see how we were doing.

Rumors went out that we had crosses in the classrooms. To the contrary, there was not one cross in the entire school section. The church and its board were more than helpful accommodating every need of ours. In fact their accommodation was more than exceptional.

The first year was not easy. I am not the type of Muslim who shows up only on Friday prayers. I am in the mosque almost daily at 6 a.m. and late at night at 9 or 10. I spent many nights sleepless thinking of how ignorant some of my fellow Muslims were. Although I tried my best not to show my emotions, I would crash emotionally when I got home, wondering why people were this way.

The local newspaper ran a story of a Muslim school in a church. Some may have thought it was strange, but, yes, Muslims and Christian can come to a common ground as we did. What Rev. McGonigle and I did was not just unique; it was building bridges.

The first year of the school was a tremendous success. Our students learned Arabic, Qur'an, Islamic studies, and a curriculum drawn from that of the Wichita public schools. To promote the school, we decided to have a graduation party in a private school in Wichita. The graduation was loud and joyous.

Preparation for the second year was more challenging. We had to add more rooms, hire more teachers and prepare the curriculum. By God's help, we were able to achieve all of that in the summer.

The next school year all of the 12 students, their brothers or sisters and many parents joined us. The second year we opened three classes: preschool, kindergarten, and first grade. During the school year many Muslim parents would visit the school to observe our progress. In my heart I was happy, because I knew the seed we had planted was blossoming. Again we had a big graduation party that enhanced the reputation of the school. For the first time, the community became exposed to children who were born in this country who now could read, write, and speak the language of the Qur'an, Arabic.

The third year was more successful. We hired more teachers, attracted more families and one-time opponents of the school became the biggest supporters. In the third year we had preschool, kindergarten, first, and second grades. By 1998 the enrollment had jumped to 51 students.

Annoor Islamic School

During all that time, I was working full time, a father, husband, principal, director, and student. Many would ask, "How can you do it?" I always said, "I sleep less, work smarter, am very committed, have a vision, and am blessed by God." Today, the school has preschool-eighth grade and is growing.

Building a bigger mosque and a community center was another stone in our community's foundation. We, "the planning committee," sat in 1995 talking about the needs of the community. Committee members agreed that we had to have a big community center that would include an Islamic school and a mosque. Having a big center that would accommodate the Muslims of Wichita would cost about $2,000,000. The main goal of the committee for the following years was to do as much fund-raising as possible.

The center was built in phases. In the first phase we raised money to build a multipurpose building and an elementary school. In the second phase, we built a mosque and a middle school. One unique observation about the Muslim community is that despite the diverse groups we have, we were able to keep the community intact. Every once in a while a spark of conflict occurs in the community, but we have succeeded in putting them out. Often I receive phone calls from individuals in our community opposing certain programs or activities just because they did not fit their criteria, yet I managed to absorb the heat for the sake of not creating harm in our community. These are blessings of God only the few has them and only the few can deal with them.

In 2000, I was selected by the community to serve as the director of the Board of Administration with the Islamic Society of Wichita for two years. This position is a sensitive one. Although we have a board to make community decisions, the director is the first to be blamed if anything goes wrong and the last to be appreciated if things go well.

My many years in Wichita and my experience, communication skills, and rich Islamic knowledge all helped me deal with many complicated issues as director of the board. Another helpful factor was that I have been very blessed with a good reputation throughout the state among Muslims and non-Muslims. Due to my public relations skills, I was selected by the Islamic Society of Wichita to be the spokesperson for the community.

In 2002 and 2004 I was again selected for two-year terms as the director of the Board of Administration. When I was asked to serve, I replied: "This is an opportunity to serve God and the community and I am honored to do it." This volunteer task is very stressful, more stressful that my own job. There are many issues I deal with daily that most of community and even board members are unaware of. I have been involved on many different levels, from helping friends all the way up to issues that may be related to immigration or government affairs.

As director, I have been involved in aspects of community and religious life, including counseling friends and husbands and wives, consulting on marriages and divorces, washing the deceased, leading the prayers, conducting Friday sermons, and speaking publicly.

As director, I have gained the trust of many brothers and sisters, Muslims and non-Muslim, but for a man in my position it is not unusual to have opponents. There is no way we can satisfy everyone.

Friday sermon

If you make one person happy, the other will be mad at you. So I have learned to satisfy God first and then evaluate everything else. The root cause of disagreements is that many Muslims don't understand Islam very well nor they have enough knowledge. To many, it is more culture than religion. Sometimes we deal with Muslims who don't even know how to read the Qur'an correctly nor understand it, yet they want to debate over a petty issue. There are some who just lay back and watch to criticize, who have not learned the Islamic virtue of saying thanks for the good works of others. As a person who delivers some of the Friday sermons, I have the opportunity to hear reactions of the audience. It is so amazing to hear that many would come and thank you for a wonderful sermon, but the same "others" always criticize. Still, one has to accept that people are different, that they are different in their levels of faith and how they apply that faith. And they are certainly different in their religious ideologies. For example, once one man called me a liberal Muslim and another called me a conservative Muslim. Although their comments were not complementary, yet as a responsible person I took the comments as a proof of my success in being a conservative and a liberal, depending on each situation.

Satisfying the others is never my goal in life. I have goals, missions, objectives, and philosophy. All I care about is satisfying God and only God. If He is pleased, I am pleased. Some people will never be happy even if you bend backward.

We are not better than the Prophets and Messengers. They went through a lot of struggles. They couldn't convince all people to follow them. We are like messengers; we have a message to deliver and a community to run. Sometimes I challenge some of the complainers to take the leadership for just a day and see how life is. Many will sit and watch the fire, but few want to extinguish it.

A friend of mine has always said, "The real leader is the one who knows how to delegate assignments." Volunteer jobs are different than corporations. Many leaders in churches would agree that finding volunteers is not an easy task. But the true leader is the one who serves his people and takes the leadership in his hands and shares responsibilities.

I view every event and action as a glass that is half-full. Some may view it has half-empty, others may view it as half-empty and half-full. It all depends on how bios we are and how we perceive issues in life. Viewing the glass half-full is a positive view, but viewing it half-empty is a negative view. With that perspective I view any event in my community as positive rather than negative.

Our community is like any other community. We have the pious and the evil; we have the good and the bad; we have the humble and the jealous; we have the angel and the envious. I am confident that all of the struggles that I have been through since childhood have taught me to stand firm before the high waves that I face daily.

Many Muslims learn Islam or become practicing Muslims in America. I learned Islam and practiced it at an early age. When I was young, I was always frequented the mosque for daily prayers. Being the director of the board makes me even more responsible to attend the prayers and oversee the demands of the community. Serving God is an opportunity only those who are fortunate may utilize correctly. I am like any Christian who is volunteering his time for the church.

Chapter 8

There's no doubt that the attacks of 9-11 were terrorist attacks. We, the Islamic Society of Wichita, were the first to issue a statement to the media condemning that evil act. The 9-11 attacks raised lots of emotions not just within the Muslim communities. You would hardly see a car without an American flag flying. Then, a few months later, the 9-11 attacks became past tense, emotions went down, and the flags were removed.

As a reaction to the 9-11 attacks, many Muslim mosques and centers were attacked across the country. Many women did not leave their homes for a long time. Some men shaved their beards, and some others considered changing their names. Many mosques and Islamic centers and schools have received hate letters and e-mails accusing them of following an evil religion.

My wife "veils" and we were in the open every night. We would go out and eat, trying to socializing with people. Once, an old man approached us with tears in his eyes as we were eating, saying, "I am sorry for the hardship you are going through. If you need any help please let me know."

Attacks on America

A man hugged me at Wal-Mart as I was walking with my wife saying, "I am proud to meet a man like you in our Wichita community. We need many people like you."

We, the Islamic Society of Wichita, have received flowers and many letters of support in addition to many positive phone calls expressing solidarity with our community. It does not mean that we did not have bad experiences. Some individuals in our community have faced challenging moments. We have been flipped-off, called names, and told to go back home.

The Islamic Society of Wichita prior to 9-11 built a very noble reputation through its dialogue with people of other faiths. We have always been proactive. But the 9-11 events opened our eyes wide open. I have always preached, "We have to get out of our confined spaces, our homes and Islamic centers, we have to open our homes and mosques to the people, and we have to socialize with the non-Muslims." If we do not, then the enemies of Islam would utilize our weakness and defame Islam without anyone to defend it.

A few days after 9-11, we opened our center to the people. We had weekly potlucks, and thousands of non-Muslims came in to have a dialogue and socialize. Since 9-11, I have been booked on Sundays and sometimes on weeknights to speak on Islam and politics throughout Kansas.

Live interviews on television

Being the spokesperson for the Islamic Society of Wichita has helped to enhance the image of our community. Daily, I was doing either live or recorded shows throughout the state. I and others have visited many of the churches in the state. Speaking about Islam was a hot item. Due to the high demand for public speakers on Islam, we tried to recruit Muslims to participate in that kind of dialogue, but very few participated. Distrust is another challenge the Muslims of America face. Many Muslims came from countries with dictatorships, where no one is allowed to say anything and spies are everywhere. So, when they come to America, that mentality does not change. They doubt you and doubt anything that is fishy. Many will not speak in public or even give an opinion. I have tried my best to persuade other Muslims to talk to the media or write letters to the editors, but fewer than five in 5,000 would do it.

Receiving the leader "angle" of the year

By the blessing of God, I have been honored by many societies and organizations over the years, especially in the aftermath of 9-11. The most honorable reward I received was the "Leader of the Year in 2002" from the community of Wichita, and most recently was presented the "2003 Community Servant Award" by the University United Methodist Church because of my active role in peace-building and multiculturalism throughout Kansas.

Nabil Seyam, Ph.D.

As a reaction to 9-11, 25 percent of Americans sought information about Islam via the Internet. In Wichita, just a few days after the 9-11 attacks, a Caucasian American Baptist woman accepted Islam in my house. In fact, many Americans have accepted Islam in Wichita and throughout the country even after 9-11. Isn't that strange?

As of a reaction to 9-11, the civil liberties of Muslim and Arab-Americans have been taken away. On Oct. 26, 2001, the Congress passed the U.S. Patriot Act, "To provide appropriate tools required to intercept and obstruct terrorism." The act gives the government new powers of detention and surveillance. It gives the secretary of state the authority to designate any group "foreign or domestic" as a terrorist organization, and that authority is not subject to review. It allows spying through wiretaps and computer surveillance; permits access to medical, financial, business, and educational records; and lets homes and offices be searched. It permits the government to detain non-citizens and to conduct secret hearings and detentions in open disregard of the court system.

As a reaction to 9-11, at least 8,000 Arab and South Asian immigrants have been interrogated because of their religion or ethnic background, not because of wrongdoing. Thousands of men, mostly Arabs and South Asians, have been held in secretive federal custody for weeks, even months, sometimes without any charges filed against them.

New attorney general guidelines allow the FBI to spy on religious and political organizations and individuals without having evidence of wrongdoing.

The fact is, security does not have to come at the expense of freedom, justice, tolerance, and equality. I and many Muslim

American do not mind any change in the law as long as it is applied to all Americans regardless of origin. But it is clear that the Patriotic Act targets Muslims and Arabs.

Just because the 9-11 attacks were carried out by Muslims and Arabs, it does not mean all Arabs and Muslims are terrorists. To balance the act, every church and white male must be spied on. That is a fair equation. If Bush campaigned in Congress to pass legislation to monitor mosques, Islamic schools, and Muslim houses due to the fact the only crime we committed was being Arabs and Muslims, then it is fair that a law must be presented to spy on all white men since Timothy McVeigh caused the Oklahoma City bombing of 1995.

The attacks of 9-11 should have made Islam the most hated religion in the world. It should have made Muslims and Arabs the most hated people in the world. However, despite the daily defaming of Islam in the American media, talk shows, and by many right-wing religious fanatics, Islam continued to be the fastest-growing religion in America.

One thing that the terrorist attacks of 9-11 did was unveil many known hypocrites among leaders. It is no secret that Arab and Muslim nations of the Middle East, Africa, and Asia have been led by dictators who care only about their thrones and wealth, and that outside powers have helped keep them at the top.

After the collapse of the Ottoman Empire, the map of the Arab and Muslim countries was drawn by the occupiers. Dividing the Middle East into tiny countries was not coincidence. It was a very well-planned scenario to weaken, divide, and create future conflicts. Some of these countries are so small they can be toured in 30 minutes.

Before the occupiers left the Middle East, they appointed dictators, kings, presidents, and sheiks that serve only their goals. Since 1948, all of the Arab leaders who came to power have been agents to their masters. They claim to be Muslims, but they are the last to know even a bit about Islam. They are seen in public praying, but they have not prayed to God one prayer. These rulers are the cause of the destruction in the Middle East and the Muslim world.

These rulers imprisoned thousands of Muslim scholars who spoke against their regimes. Thousands of men and women have been in prisons for over 40 years. Many of the terrorist cells that exist today are a breed of generations that have been under occupation in their own countries.

The only true elected leaders in the Middle East are the leaders of Lebanon, Iran, and Palestine. The rest have been in power since the birth of civilization.

President Bush is calling upon Arab nations to have democratic states. How can they have democratic states if freedom is forbidden and no one is allowed to speak up? All sorts of media are controlled by the government. Even Islamic scholars who work for the government are agents for the leaders. They do not fear God; they fear their masters.

Bush's call for democracy in the Middle East is a joke. Bush and all Arab and Muslim leaders know what would happen if democracy were granted. The people would pick religious leaders who rule by the Qur'an and the teaching of Prophet Mohammad, peace be upon him. Would the Arab leaders, Bush, and the European nations be happy?

The terrorist attacks of 9-11 were carried out by Saudi citizens. Why the U.S. did not retaliate against Saudi Arabia? Are oil interests more important than the moral obligation of facing the real attackers?

Bush attacked Afghanistan because the Saudi hijackers were trained in Afghanistan and Al-Qaida is based there. Is it fair to retaliate against a whole nation for the acts of the few? We have killed more Afghani civilians in Afghanistan than Al-Qaida members. No, this is not the price of war; this is the price of wrong judgment. You cannot get to Saudi Arabia through Afghanistan.

Saudi Prince

The same is true of Iraq. Who is the bad guy, the Iraqis or Saddam? Sure, Saddam is. Then why are we humiliating the Iraqis, mainly the prisoners? We have treated Iraqis worse than Saddam did. At least Saddam's brutal history was known. He never called for human rights or for

Bush

a free democracy. He never admitted that he was a man of values. The immoral act of some of the American soldiers in Iraq was reviled by God. How many other Muslim POWs have been raped or killed by American soldiers? I am not claming that the Arabs or the Muslims have noble soldiers. But the fact, is, none of the Arab

and the Muslim countries have claimed that they are human right activists, that they care at all about the human rights, that they are the leaders of the free world or masters of democracy.

We have to walk the talk. This administration has defamed and humiliated the entire Muslim and Arab nations due to the acts of

Saddam

a few Saudis. For Bush to go on Arab television trying to sanitize the image of the American soldiers is not beneficial. He can influence Arab leaders but not the Arab people.

Muslims and Islam have been defamed for the actions of a few. Yet, when the few of the American soldiers committed indecent acts in the Iraqi prisons, the administration defended the entire army and said, "Those few soldiers do not represent all Americans; that was not an American VALUE."

President Bush declared "You are either with us or with them." This statement is short but has many meanings: The whole world either supports Bush, right or wrong, otherwise you are an enemy. Bush's statement led the dictators and hypocrites of the world to stand with him because they didn't want to be the enemy, nor did they want to lose their throne and the wealth it generates.

Unfortunately, some of the practices of Middle East dictatorships have come to America under Bush: The if-you're-not-with-me, you're-against-me attitude and the disregard for what the world community thinks.

Bush may be able to remove the leader of all dictators, Saddam, but he cannot remove the nations. Where was the free world when Saddam poisoned and killed thousands of his own people? Where was the whole world when Hafez Assad committed massacres in Syria? What about the torture of innocent people in the prisons of Israel, Jordan, Syria, Saudi Arabia, and Egypt? Why did no one raise a voice? What about the daily terrorist attacks by Israeli forces on Palestinian civilians? Aren't they people like us in America? It is a shame that when Kuwait was invaded, the whole world was united to free the oil — I mean to free Kuwait. Is oil more precious than human life? By what book do they rule?

Hafez Assad

When Saddam was torturing and killing his own people, he was the most beloved leader to the United Nations and the rest of the world. It is because he was doing his masters a favor, killing Iranians and trying to defeat a new Muslim leadership led by Ayatullah Ruhollah Khomeini.

Yasser Arafat

Yasser Arafat had been considered the No. 1 terrorist since the seventies. Overnight he became the man of peace and, on top of that, received a Nobel Prize,

Even Moammar Qadafi of Libya became a hero overnight, and sanctions against his country were lifted. Who makes these decisions? Who has the power to change the minds of the world's nations? Who is behind-the-scenes power

that determines who is the good guy and who is the bad guy?

The reasons given for the occupation of Iraq — seeking weapons of mass destruction, removing Saddam, hunting down Al-Qaida — are nothing but propaganda. We are losing American soldiers daily for what reason? The

Qadafi

oil? Son avenging his father? Avenging the 9-11 attacks? To show patriotism?

The American people deserve an honest answer. For Bush to gain respect of the American people and the world, he needs to improve his style of administration.

Ahmad Chalabi (the Iraqi Council Member who is paid by American taxpayers up to $340,000 a month) had told the U.S. government, "The Iraqis will receive you with roses." Where are the roses? What happened to the joy that Iraqi had when Saddam's statue was removed? Now we have discovered that Ahmad Chalabi lied and used the Bush administration for his own goals, to become Iraq's president. How could such a man wanted by the Jordanian government for theft fool the president of the greatest country in the world?

I, who do not have a degree in political science, could have told Bush that Chalabi is a crook. I am shocked that this crook can fool the Bush administration.

The New York Times said its reporting in a number of stories leading up to the war in Iraq and the early occupation "was not as rigorous as it should have been." Again, who is imbedding stories and isn't it too late to unveil it?

The White House blames the FBI for wrong intelligence information, the FBI blames the CIA, the British government blames others, Bush blames Chalabi, and others blame others. For God's sake, who is to blame for faulty information? Well, let's look at it this way. Who benefits the most because of the war in Iraq? It's the one who provided the "unintelligent" information.

Secretary of Defense Donald Rumsfeld's claim that the supporters of Saddam and Al-Qaida are those who are fighting the American efforts in Iraqi is far from the truth. We have to admit that Iraqi civilians are fighting back, that they are resisting the occupation.

Rumsfeld's

Rumsfeld and other representatives have to stand up and face the truth and admit that something is not going right in Iraq.

Many Iraqis feel that the situation during the occupation is worse than during Saddam. Iraqis view the U.S. forces as occupiers not liberators. No doubt many Iraqis are happy that Saddam was removed, but they are not happy that they are jobless, unsafe, imprisoned, tortured, humiliated, homeless, naked, raped, defamed, and that their religious buildings have been destroyed.

It is a shame that to this day the United Nations cannot define the word terrorism. Why? Well, look at the occupation of Palestine and the Palestinians. Look at the daily killing of civilians in the West Bank and Gaza. Tens of houses are destroyed daily. Palestine is the only occupied land in the world. Isn't the act of the Israeli government a form of terrorism? Who has the right to call the civilian Palestinian who is defending his land a guerrilla but the Israeli soldier who drives tanks is a freedom fighter? Who makes these standards and on what basis?

When I came back to Wichita in 1990, I was shocked to see and hear that the Iraqi army was the third-largest in the world, that it had more than a million soldiers and thousands of tanks and planes. It was

demolition houses   Beating a child

all lies. I witnessed the invasion of Kuwait. Iraqi men were forced to invade Kuwait after an eight-year war with Iran. Iraqi soldiers told us, "We are not here to fight. Kuwaitis are our uncles and cousins." Many Iraqi soldiers went to Kuwait walking barefoot for days in 120-plus-degree heat. The people in Kuwait fed the soldiers, who were left in the desert of Kuwait with no food or drinks. Saddam had put the Shiite Muslims in the front line of the battle, while he kept his Sunni Muslims protected in Baghdad. The U.S. and the allied forces during the liberation of Kuwait did Saddam a big favor: They killed the Shiite Muslims. Iraqi soldiers had the same clothes for months, no showers or bathrooms facilities. Many of the soldiers carried their own old rifles.

Why is it that in the first Gulf War the troops stopped near Baghdad? Was it to protect Saddam's forces? Or was it a preparation for Chapter 2 of the Gulf War? Is it a series? What is next? Is it politics? To tell us that the mission was to liberate Kuwait and only to liberate Kuwait was an old joke. Kuwait was invaded by one man, you remove the man, and Kuwait will be liberated. Saddam drove his own Mercedes coming from Baghdad all the way to Kuwait. Why did the UNITED STATES not get rid of him then?

Who made Saddam? Did not Rumsfeld meet with him? During their friendship, Saddam was torturing and killing his own people. Was he slapped on the hand or was our ally told "good job"?

Rumsfeld and Saddam

Who made Osama Bin Laden and who supported him for years during the Soviet Union invasion of Afghanistan? Didn't the UNITED STATES help Bin Laden?

Why many of us like to put our heads in the dirt and act like we don't see or hear anything. Isn't it the meaning of democracy to say what you believe is right?

Many Muslims in the Middle East and throughout the world believe that Bush's war in Afghanistan and Iraq is a war on Islam.

Osama Bin Laden

The triangle of evil that was drawn by Bush has been perpetrated as an evil triangle because they did not obey his majesty, President Bush. Any leader or individual who does not support Bush is going to be put on the evil list or called un-American. Now, the longtime dictator, Qadafi of Libya, is an example of a man of courage. He is no longer an evil man ... why?

Each and every Arab leader is a copy of Saddam. The only difference is that Saddam has a big mouth and is crazy. Show me one Arab prison that is free of humiliation and punishment. Go to Saudi Arabia, Syria, Libya, Morocco, Algeria, Tunisia, Egypt, and elsewhere. Their prisons are human slaughterhouses. Do you know why Arab leaders, including Musharaf of Pakistan, did not condemn the actions of American soldiers in the prison of Abu Ghraib? Because they do worse, that's why. The only difference is that their prisons do not have cameras; they have saws that cut people alive.

We are living in an era full of evils and evilness. You are either with them or against them. Even many U.S. senators and representatives cannot speak against the president freely because they would be called unpatriotic. This is the new dictatorship that Bush has invented in America. Unfortunately, the disease of the Arab leaders has spread to U.S. politics.

Arab leaders have taken advantage of the terrorist attacks on 9-11 and started to obey their masters by accusing the Islamic organizations of being Al-Qaida or at least having connection to Al-Qaida. Any bombing is blamed on Al-Qaida anymore. This reminds me of the police department that couldn't solve the crime and finally they start accusing a "serial killer" just to claim they were on the killer's trail. Arab leaders are facing great opposition from many Islamic organizations, which have been opposed by the governments for years. Now they have a great opportunity to fight them by accusing them of collaborating with Al-Qaida. The price of politics is expensive.

Many Muslims believe that Arab and Muslim leaders, who have fought Muslim activists for years, have gained U.S. blessings by turning against activist Muslims or killing them. This type of condition will not last forever. In fact, Arab leaders have pushed the Arabs and the Muslims in their countries to the edge. It is only a matter of time before things will turn upside down.

Some Arab leaders don't even know how to read Arabic or recite verses of the Holy Qur'an. Isn't it a shame that these people are in control of the wealth of the Muslim Nation? I was so angry to hear the Crown Prince of Saudi Arabia reading verses of the Holy Qur'an wrong from a paper he had. But the fact has to be said, "When the worst leads you, know that you are even worse" because you allow yourself to be led by the likes of them.

(Saudi Crown Prince)

Countries like Pakistan and Afgh-anistan have closed many Islamic schools due to pressure from the United States, accusing these schools of teaching violence. It is amazing, saying that the Holy Qur'an teaches violence. For God's sake, who makes these determinations? Every time they close a school in a Muslim country, God replaces it by another school in Canada, England, France, or the United States.

The entire Middle East is a time bomb. People are under a lot of stress due to government pressure, imprisonment of relatives, spying, restrictions, and the lack of free expression. In some Muslim countries, an individual who frequents the mosque is questioned by authorities.

Anything that happens in the Middle East will affect the entire world. Therefore, the United States must think seriously about its foreign policy. Otherwise the American people will continue to pay for mistakes caused by the government.

Countries like Egypt and Jordan are paid billions of dollars in "blackmail" to skew decisions at the Arab summits to protect their assets. The Middle East has not had an honest leader since 1948. All of them are corrupt; all of them are rats.

Husni Mubarak   King Husain

Bush claims that this war is against terrorism. If this is true, terrorism should have decreased. The war in Iraq and Afghanistan has caused many sleepy cells to wake up and fight us Americans. Whether we like it or not, America will end up paying the price. Is this fair? Is it fair that Americans are killed? We need to remember that we were attacked by Saudi citizens and not Iraqi or Afghani citizens.

The American people are nice and humble and have many Islamic values that many of the Muslims have lost. The main problem with many Americans is that they are relaxed. I'm not trying to be negative, but I am trying to be honest. Many Americans have been brainwashed day after day through a little tube called TV.

Most Americans receive their information either through newspapers, TV, or talk shows. Many Americans live a relaxed life. They lie on recliners, drinking soda while receiving the news. We don't see many curious people that would go beyond this little biased tube. The media has always defamed Muslims and Islam. This is not unusual. Native Americans, blacks, Germans, and Japanese went through it. We are not special. However, we are the first to be attacked for our faith. We have daily crimes in Wichita and in the United States, but I have never heard the media saying, "A Christian man was shot to death by another Christian." Or "A Baptist woman was robbed by a Catholic." A Texas man was sentenced to 11 years in prison for having weapons of mass destruction. What was his faith? What was his race or color? They were not a factor. Why?

Many Americans are either Republicans or Democrats, and each party believes it is the only true party. Many Americans blindly follow either party, basing their actions on what the media tells them. In 2000 I voted as Republican, but in 2004 I will vote as Democrat. We have to be moderate and follow who we believe may help America. To be radical for a party and fight for it despite its wrong judgment is not helpful.

When it comes to an act of a Muslim, it will be in a big headline screaming "Extremist Muslim kills 5 civilians." This is exactly what the enemies of Islam want the whole world to think of Muslims and Islam, that Muslims follow an evil religion. Americans need to reject this spreading disease. Is it fair that I take unedited tape of Jerry Springer to the Middle East and show it on public television saying, "If you need to know inside America, watch this." Is this a fair comparison? A veiled Muslim woman is looked upon as abused, but a Catholic woman who is veiled is pious. A Muslim man with a beard is a terrorist, but a Christian man with a beard is a religious person.

Why we never hear about the faith of Terry Nichols? Or is it because he is not Muslim it does not matter? Some people rejected that the attacks on Oklahoma were committed by a white American, that it was impossible. White Americans cannot do such an act. Timothy McVeigh and Terry Nichols must have had relationship with an Arab or a Muslim. This reminds me of when I first came to Kansas in 1980. People would tell me, "Do not live in a black neighborhood; they are bad people." This stereotype is nothing but a virus is carried by people who themselves are sick.

The illness does not stop with the media. It is seen even in many churches. Some ministers have taken advantage of the terrorist attacks on America to defame Islam and the Prophet Mohammad during their Sunday sermons.

I watched an entire sermon on a local channel in Wichita of a reverend defaming Islam and spreading lie after lie about the faith. Usually our reaction is to pray for these people. We always ask God to guide them and we ask Him to have them walk their talk.

Rumsfeld and others are leading a war against Al-Jazeera, an Arab television station based in Qatar. The attack on Al-Jazeera is solid evidence that the world media is controlled by the few. We have to hear, listen, and read only the Rumsfeld media information. Any other media that opposes the U.S. media is biased. Rumsfeld himself attacked Al-Jazeera due to the fact that Al-Jazeera not following the line that is drawn to the world media. Is this the democracy of Rumsfeld? Is this the new freedom? You either relay what we say or you are an enemy. With most radio and television stations controlled by a handful of individuals, the media has the power to manipulate and control people's thinking, but enough is enough. There has to be another channel that relays the truth from now on. It is about time that, in the Middle East a channel like Al-Jazeera relays facts as seen. The question I would like to leave you with, who is in control of the media in America?

As a result of the occupation of Iraqi, more attacks have been occurring throughout the whole world. That was an expected reaction of unjust war. Because of Bush's leadership, we Americans have become the least respected people in the world. Bush claims he has destroyed the network of the terrorists. The truth is that Bush has awakened many terrorist cells, and now they are taking advantage of this mentality to spread fear all over the world. This war and occupation have bred generations full of hatred to America. Bush will go away and we, the American people, will continue paying the price.

a rock and a tank

Being the supreme power in the world should have given us the advantage to spread peace and freedom. America should be respected not feared.

Spreading democracy or freedom with force has never worked. Look at what we can learn from the Palestinian-Israeli conflict. Palestine was occupied in 1948, and in 1967 the West Bank and Gaza were also occupied. Generations after generations were born after the occupation of Palestine, and those generations are more solid than a rock in their opposition to Israel. Despite the torture in Israeli prisons, demolition of houses, the killing of men and women with American weapons, Palestinians still fight for their liberation. The world community does not understand the mentality of Arabs. Arabs prefer to die in dignity than to live in shame.

Israeli soldier aiming his machinegun

The United States has taken a role to help Israel with all of its power. That is great. However, justice has to be served. The Palestinians are more that 8 million people. They cannot be neglected. They are a nation like any other nation. All Arabs and Muslim view Jerusalem and Palestine as holy places. This is an Islamic belief. Regardless of who owns the land today, we, as the supreme power, must respect the feeling of others and play the role of peacekeepers.

Israeli soldier aiming his machinegun

We must admit that the root cause of the conflict in the Middle East is the Palestinian-Israeli conflict. If we can solve this conflict, terrorism will disappear from the region. However, as long as the U.S. government is taking sides, tension will continue and each one of us living in America will be affected by the results.

Public speaking throughout Kansas

Chapter 9

Since the terrorist attacks of 9-11, Muslims and non-Muslims have been spending a lot of their energy interpreting their understanding of the concept of Jihad. Many clergy members have become scholars and have spent sermons explaining to non-Muslims the concept of Jihad, which has mistakenly been interpreted as "holy war." Jihad can be utilized as a good or a bad act depending on the Islamic knowledge of the presenter or the reporter of the concept.

Once, while giving a lecture, a woman from the audience asked what Jihad meant. To answer her question I asked her a question: "What would your reaction be if I say to you that I am gay?" She said, "Nothing, this is your lifestyle and I cannot be involved in your personal life." I said, "That's exactly what I thought you would say." I said the word gay means happy. In the English language the word gay means I am happy. So it depends on whom, how, and when you use it. The same is true of Jihad.

To understand the concept of Jihad, we must understand the meaning of the word. Jihad is an Arabic word that means to struggle, to seek self-improvement, to derive solutions, to come closer to God, and to fight oppression.

The teacher who struggles in class daily is conducting a form of Jihad, the mother or father who suffers bad treatment and disrespect from their children is in a form of Jihad, and the believer who lives a godly life where evil surrounds him or her is in Jihad. To be a good pious person is a form of Jihad and to defend yourself is a form of Jihad.

Once Mohammad and the companions were coming from a battlefield, and he said to the people, "Now we came back from the minor Jihad to the major Jihad." He meant life.

Jihad cannot be declared by a group or individuals; it has to be declared by the Islamic state. Out of more than 54 Muslim countries, none has ever declared Jihad.

In Islam fighting is forbidden unless it is for self-defense. If the enemy calls for peace, peace should be accepted. Islam is the religion of peace and peace is the basis of all human relations.

In Islam, prisoner of war rights must be protected. They must be provided food, shelter, and clothing. It is forbidden in Islam to mistreat or punish a prisoner of war. But Islam has gone further than that, defining a prisoner of war as a prisoner of the state, not as a prisoner of his captives.

There are strict rules of war in Islam that must be abided regardless of who you are fighting. A Muslim cannot destroy a religious building and civil buildings, cut a tree, or kill non-combatants or livestock. If a combatant turns his back, a Muslim cannot kill him. What is so fascinating about Islam is that whatever has been prohibited during peace has also been prohibited during war.

The term holy war does not exist in Islam. In fact, this term was invented to associate Islam with it. Islam was never spread by the sword. To the contrary, no one can be forced to accept Islam; one has to choose it freely.

Jihad, war, Islam, and holy are terms that are misunderstood by many Muslims and non-Muslims. If you don't understand the Arabic language and the explanation behind verses of the Qur'an and the reasons behind the revealing of these verses, then you have no right to neither criticize the Qur'an nor quote it. The whole Qur'an must be taken as a text to understand it.

Al-Qaida, Taliban, and other Islamic groups misunderstand the interpretations of the verses of the Holy Qur'an. I believe with all of my heart that those groups believe that what they are doing is 100 percent Islamic. Many of the millions of Muslims who have supported or sympathized with Osama Bin Laden have commiserated with him because of the struggles they face in their own countries. Unfortunately, many Muslims follow their emotions instead of their brains when it comes to acts such as those committed by Bin Laden... Muslims are waiting for someone to free them from the slavery of the Arab dictators and unfortunately they believe that Osama is the man. I recall back in 1990 during the invasion of Kuwait, when Saddam said today Kuwait, tomorrow Israel. Surely, many Arabs were excited when they heard words like that, even though Saddam was playing games and trying to manipulate people's feelings. Another way to move the Arabs' emotions is through telling them that we will abide by the Islamic law. Saddam declared that he would cut off the hand of thieves. He did. However, he also cut off the tongues and ears of people, but that's not Islamic law. Again, this is one of many tools Saddam and other Arab leaders use to move emotions.

I personally believe that the actions of the Taliban and Al-Qaida were not Islamic acts. For sharing that view around some Muslims, it made me appear unfaithful. You will find Muslims who condemn or condone his attacks on America. It all depends on the level of knowledge and the environment.

History, whether Islamic or non-Islamic, is full of incidents that were driven by religion. Slaughtering people alive is not a strange act. Read history. What's strange is that now with all of the technology we have today, we all can see it. In the old days it was mostly unseen. The slaughter of the innocent young American in Iraq was filmed, but I did not have the stomach to watch it. The last time I saw a man been slaughtered was in an email attachment that showed a Muslim Chechnyan man being slaughtered by a Russian soldier. I couldn't eat or drink for a week.

It is sad that many talk-show hosts spend many hours doing nothing except slandering Islam and Muslims, because their agenda is to keep the American public misinformed about the true face of Islam.

After the terrorist attacks of 9-11 on America, many religious leaders and talk radio hosts had established that these attacks were attacks on America and Christians. The latest bombings in Saudi Arabia proved the opposite. Al-Qaida has declared that any government that cooperates with the United States government is a wanted government. Saudi Arabia is one of the major supporters of the United States, although observers in the media may not see it that way. What was so surprising to the Saudi government is that after every attack in the kingdom, they discovered that the attacks were conducted by individuals who were not known to the government, that the ranks of their opponents seem to grow and grow. This is a major problem not just to the Saudi government but also to the United States because Al-Qaida is recruiting thousands of new members.

In a statement on Al-Jazeera, an Al-Qaida member said, "This is a war in Saudi Arabia until the last infidel leaves" Saudi Arabia. This is a powerful statement, meaning that this is a war that will last a long time.

Many Muslims believe that all Arab leaders, including the Saudi regime, are unbelievers. The common people as well as the Muslim scholars have differences of opinion on that issue. If a group believes leaders are hypocrites and unbelievers, then their philosophy is to destroy that leader and any power that helps him. But we see that other Muslims, including some scholars, believe that no one can call a Muslim unbeliever unless there is a clear sign.

One of the major problems in the Muslim countries is that they have allowed the very strict version of Islam to prosper and have tried to contain the moderate version of Islam. This was done intentionally by Arab leaders. For the whole world to hear the true face of Islam, they need to do the following:

- Remove discrimination from the heart.
- Remove favoritism from the heart.
- Read Islamic books that are written by moderate scholars.
- Go to my web site, **www.seyam.org**, for more information

Personally, I predict the increase of nasty explosions all over the world but specifically Saudi Arabia, since Al-Qaida has more supporters in Saudi than any other country. Being a man who was raised and lived in the Middle East and has studied the history of existing and past Arab leaders I could share the following statement

Nabil Seyam, Ph.D.

with comfort: ***In this era we are paying the price of many years of oppression and transgressions of the past.***

We need to view every terrorist attack whether it was conducted by an individual or a group as an act independent of the faith even if the attacks were done in the name of religion. Adolf Hitler, Timothy McVeigh, David Koresh, and others do not represent the white man or Christianity; Bin Laden, Saddam, and the Taliban do not represent all Muslims or Islam. The same goes with treating the holy verses of the Qur'an. Just as many talk-show hosts and clergy quote verses from the Qur'an that suggest a violent act, I could quote hundreds of Bible verses that do the same.

For example, in Leviticus 20:27: "And as for man or woman in whom there proves to be a mediumistic spirit or spirit of prediction, they should be put to death without fail. They should pelt them to death with stones. Their own blood is upon them"

And Numbers 31:17-18: "Now therefore kill every male among the little ones, and kill every woman that hath known man by lying with him. But all the women children, that have not known a man by lying with him, keep alive for yourselves."

Read Judges 16:27-30, and 15:14-16, Numbers 31:31-40 and 21:32-35 and 21:2-3 and 31:17-18, and 25:1-9. The list can go on and on.

It is absurd to call Islam the unpeaceful religion. The sad part is that those who deprecate Islam themselves are not idols to follow. Unfortunately, many of them are trying to use the emotions of the American people for their own benefit.

104

Chapter 10

S addam has ruined the lives of millions of people. After the liberation of Kuwait, the United Nations compensated all residents and citizens of Kuwait who had lost assets due to the invasion. The compensation came as an agreement with the Iraqi government through selling oil.

Many American hostages have filed lawsuits against Saddam and his regime. I hired a law firm in Washington, D.C., to represent me for claims against the Republic of Iraq, the Iraqi Intelligence Service, and Saddam Hussein. The papers were filled with the United States District Court for the District of Columbia.

Although the claim is for the amount of $104 million, there is no cap on the value of a human life. I did not sue Saddam until the collapse of his regime. Being an Arab-American and suing Saddam during his life is worse than just being an American. I seriously believed that if I had sued Saddam while he was in power, I would have been killed. Therefore, the collapse of his regime was a great opportunity.

I was very disappointed to hear that some Muslims in my own community were talking ill behind my back because of the legal action. "Nabil should have not sued Saddam; the money is Iraqi money, and Islamically, it is forbidden," some would say. What is so sad is that some individuals don't understand that we are living in a world full of laws to protect the value of human beings. No money can bring back the life of a human. But money is the only compensation for what has been taken.

To act as an Islamic scholar and make such interpretations about my actions is unIslamic. A Muslim published a newsletter and distributed it in our community telling people what Nabil is doing is wrong. This and many issues are some of the struggles I and others are facing within our own communities. These are personal matters that touch feelings and should be respected. Life had taught me that it's not what you do, it's who does it. If you are liked, anything you do will be approved. If you are not liked, nothing will be approved.

The politics of Bush is involved in everything, including the lawsuit. Bush has stated that the United States is in the middle of working with the new government of Iraq, so how can we make legal claims against "our friends."

Our lawyers have not given up hope that a resolution could come soon.

I was held a hostage because I am a U.S. citizen. That was my crime. I was accused of being a spy, falsely imprisoned, tortured, assaulted, and battered by officials of the Republic of Iraq. The treatment while in the control of the Iraqi Intelligence Service personnel was particularly barbarous. This torture produced severe pain and suffering, both physical and mental, and was intentionally inflicted by the Intelligence Service. I suffered agonizing physical pain and intense and prolonged mental anguish and harm, both during the actual torture and throughout captivity.

My former wife, children, and parents suffered severe mental anguish as a result of the kidnapping and detention, and as a result of Iraqi's denial that I was held as a hostage, leaving them to imagine the horrors I must be enduring.

Chapter 11

Muslims understand and realize that Islam is a monotheistic religion. It is protected not by Arabs or Muslims; it is protected by God Himself. With that perspective, Muslims should not concentrate on how much Islam is defamed in the media; rather they should concentrate on living an Islamic life.

Muslims of America have realized the importance of building Islamic schools, which are producing a Muslim American generation that will be able to communicate, act, and react with American society. Muslims have realized that in order to make it in America and in order to compete with the daily struggle that we face, we must be involved in American politics. This new generation is breeding new Muslim American lawyers who understand the system. In order for American Muslims to succeed in America, they have to understand the language. We are talking about the language of politics. We have many Muslim Americans who are doctors, engineers, and entrepreneurs, but we don't have many that are lawyers.

Muslims of America need to practice the moderate type of Islam and stay away from fanatic interpretations. God says in the Holy Qur'an, "We have made you a moderate nation." Extremisms, terrorisms, and radicalisms should not exist in Islam. Islam is a peaceful religion and calls others for peace.

Muslims of America voted for Bush in 2000 believing that he was the man who was going to make life better for them. However, Muslims have been betrayed by Bush and his policies, so the majority will not vote for him in 2004. We, as Muslim Americans, need to

107

educate our community about the importance of voting. Many have come from countries where elections are not known, so voting is not a habit. Other Muslims believe that neither party is going to help the Muslim American cause, so why should we vote? Many Muslim Americans believe that Democrats and Republicans are two faces of the same coin, making voting a waste of time. Muslim Americans understand that they are targeted because of their beliefs and national origin.

Some successful Muslim Americans have been accused of crimes or questioned as a material witness for crimes they did not commit. Brandon Mayfield is a living example of that. An American who converted to Islam, Mayfield is a lawyer and married to an Egyptian. He was one of the suspects in the deadly Madrid train station bombing, picked up by the FBI, jailed, and tagged as a terrorist in his own country. The FBI soon learned that it was wrong and set him free. Their apology will not bring back his life. Once you are labeled you are tagged forever.

Focusing on groups or individuals based on their religion or national origin alone is not the American way. That's not what America was founded upon. If Bin Laden and his group committed a crime, go after them. But going after professional Muslims who have decided to take this land as their home is not right. If the war is not against Islam and Muslims, then why are Muslims in America spied upon? Why are Muslims pinpointed? Why are mosques bugged?

America speaks loud when it comes to free speech and human rights. I do not believe this is the case when it comes to Muslim Americans. A white man can criticize this country day and night, and he will be looked at as a man expressing his opinion. But if a Muslim American says the same words or criticizes America, he will be detained and accused of being with Al-Qaida. Democracy in America is a selective one. It depends on one's race and faith. Still, I agree that America has some form of democracy. Democracy is not known in the Middle East.

We, the Muslim Americans, exemplify many long-held American values. We are living in a country in harmony and peace, practicing our faith freely. This land has hugged us and taken us in as citizens. On a personal level, I am the spokesperson for the community who is on record with the local newspaper stating, "If a terrorist is within our community, I will turn him in to the government." We have Islamic obligations to stop evil acts. The harm will not come from us; the harm will come from those who want to create ill in the American society for the purpose of dividing us. We should all be aware of this and be united, as we were united before and during the struggle of 9-11. This world is full of evil and if we, the people, fall in the trap of politicians then we all will lose.

We will keep seeing pictures of "suspected terrorist MUSLIMS" all over the media, claiming that these individuals are plotting an attack on America. Depending on the reader, we all may have different interpretations. Democrats may view it as a way to steer attention away from problems in Iraq and Afghanistan. Republicans may view it as a way to tell the American people, "We have told you, something was going to happen." And the Muslims got stuck with both parties. We became the beating boys. We became a tool to scare the American people. If you want to raise the alert level, all you have to do is present images of Arabs and Muslims on national television and the job is done.

The power of the media in America is not something that can be ignored. We are talking about brainwashing and skewing the opinions of billions of people. Therefore, the image of an Arab or a Muslim will continue to unfold in the media for years to come. Therefore, Muslims in America and Europe will suffer tremendous humiliations for a long time. I and others see it and live it.

America needs to return to its origins. We need to be loved and respected rather than hated and feared. America should be the leader of all countries, not the follower of traces of a shadow. We may be able to interfere in all of the world problems, but we need to fix our own first. The lifestyles of Americans have changed dramatically in the past four years.

As the color of threat levels change, people's stress changes, too. Is this what we want, to live in fear in our own homes? Not one day passes without an American being killed outside the United States. Is it fair that our troops are spread thin in over 40 countries? We cannot police ever country in the world. Let's learn from the experience of "small Britain." We need America to have the peace we had prior to 9-11.

President Carter

I have always said if former President Carter were our president today, the Palestinian-Israeli conflict would have been solved by now. American foreign policy in the Middle East has been a failure since the end of the Carter administration. Carter's wisdom is needed nowadays, because Bush's style does not work in today's world. We are dealing with cells that are willing to burn anything that moves, and we must be wiser in dealing with them. I am not suggesting giving up, but I am suggesting that we review the cause of the evil in the world. Why do we have conflicts? Let's get to the root cause instead of trying to

President Carter

cure just the symptoms. Our foreign policy failure has led to the chaos that we are in today. I hate to see that we are fighting like kids, with me hitting him because he hit me.

We have to sit down and ask ourselves why the 9-11 attacks occurred. What truly caused it? What can we do to prevent future attacks? If we don't seriously answer these questions, then the 9-11 attacks will keep occurring. The issue is not securing the airports, tunnels, and the White House. It is securing the American people and it is for Americans to feel secure everywhere in the world. Today, Americans cannot travel without being targeted. This is something no power can secure except the power of the brain, of wisdom, of justice, and of equality. We can spend billion of dollars securing our borders and bugging every building in America, but if a terrorist wants to commit a crime it can be done. Look at the prisons of America for an example of the law being unable to prevent crime. Let me share another logical example: If people are committing sins under the watch of God Himself, how can we think they would stop?

The answer is peace. Let's do our best as a supreme power to spread peace in the world. The American democracy may work here, but it cannot be forced upon the Middle East. I came from there and I know it does not work. In psychology, I always learned that each human has three essential needs above all others: food, shelter, and clothing. The entire leadership of the Middle East must change to acquire democracy. The leaders are not trusted and as long as they are in power nothing will be achieved, including meeting those essential needs.

The American government needs not to take sides. The power that the United States has today is a power that has been granted by God. Let's not abuse it. Let's look back, where are the empires of Egypt, Rome, Persia, Islam, and the USSR? They are all gone. We need to remember that no bird will fly forever; one day it will come down. Knowing that, leaders of nations must fear God. They must know that one day we will face Him, and we will be responsible for every act we've done in this life. The Muslim leader Omar once said, "If a sheep was lost in Iraq, God will ask me about it. He will ask if I have paved the way for it."

America looks like a beautiful tree that has lots of fruits, however it's roots are rotten and is about to destroy the whole tree. Many of the American people are living their days but forgetting that death is approaching. The society is full of decay and immorality to the point if you condemn it, you would be criticized. Read the books of God and understand how and why other nations were destroyed, because of morality.

Presidents, sheiks, kings, and prime ministers will be judged first in the judgment day because they have more responsibilities than us. God will say, "Where are the Kings?" Many leaders may play the game of politics today, looking for what is best for their agenda. But tomorrow they will face the creator one on one. We will all die tomorrow and take no wealth or title with us to the grave. The only thing we'll take is our deeds. "So whosoever does good equal to the weight of an atom shall see it, and whosoever does evil equal to the weight of an atom shall see it," the Holy Qur'an says. We ask God to guide our leaders to benefit humanity and to spread peace in the world.

Nabil with Kansas Governor Bill Graves

Nabil & Susan with Scott Ritter, U.N. weapons
inspector to Iraq

Nabil with Secretary of State Dan Glickman

Nabil with Dr. Douglas Markham, author and expert
in nutritional counseling

What the leaders say about Dr. Seyam

Dr. Seyam has been a strong motivator of communication in the Wichita community between followers of the Muslim faith and the community at large, especially in the wake of 9/11. As leader of the Islamic Society of Wichita, he has initiated open meetings and discussions by graciously opening the Wichita Islamic Center to all for food, fellowship, and talking about 9/11 issues that should be of concern to every community. Dr. Seyam has also given stimulating and edifying talks at many other community venues, such as universities, churches and social centers in Wichita. His message is consistently one of challenging assumptions on all sides · and encouraging constructive dialog toward conciliation.

Armin Gerhard, Wichita State University

Nabil Seyam is one of those unique high energy "take charge" individuals who identifies problems or gaps in situations and redefines them as opportunities. He then looks at how he personally can affect the outcome and begins putting into place the solution while the rest of us are still talking. Anyone reading this book will be inspired by his persistence to overcome the many obstacles life has placed in front of him.

Robbie Cline, CPIW, CPCU, M.S. Ed.

I first became acquainted with Dr. Nabil Seyam as a member of a professional organization of safety engineers (ASSE) and was initially impressed by his commitment to professionalism. As I got to know him better, I became aware of his knowledge of the field and his dedication to the improvement of the quality and standards of the profession. After Nabil became an educational colleague, I learned about his background both personal and professional that prepared him with a unique basis to view a situation that allows him to more fully understand events, situations, and cause/effect relationships. Knowing Dr. Seyam as a professional safety engineer, educator, researcher, philosopher, and friend has enriched both my personal and professional life.

Dr. Ray Denton, Pittsburg State University

Long before 9-11, Nabil Seyam saw a mission to build bridges between his Muslim community and the community of Kansas. He has spent countless hours speaking to various groups. He arranged pot luck dinners at the Muslim Community Center which were open to the public. He participated in a public television project that educated the viewers about the different ethnic groups in Wichita. His vision, objectivity, empathy, balance, and sincere love of mankind are unsurpassed.

Marie Gillespie, The East Wichita Shepherd's center

Nabil is a friend of mine and I believe he is an important bridge between the culture of our community.

Bob Knight, Wichita Mayor

Nabil Seyam has invaluable insight for our ever-emerging global society. His incredible experiences and deep passion speak not only to our generation but have implications for the future - politically, religiously, and personally. Nabil has been a founding leader for the Islamic tradition in Wichita while providing a foundation for dialog and cooperation in the wider interfaith community."

Rev. Dr. Robin McGonigle

Dr. Nabil Seyam's positive leadership and dedication has been a tremendous asset for the City of Wichita. He has been in the forefront of building and fostering partnerships between citizens and law enforcement in our community.

Norman D. Williams, Wichita Chief of Police

When the Kansas Institute for Peace and Conflict Resolution, as a part of its annual Peace Lecture Series, sought to develop community events focused on Muslim/Christian relations, Nabil Seyam was key to its success. Despite a very busy schedule, Nabil was the primary representative of the Muslim community for planning, a speaker in the series itself, and a proponent of this and ongoing dialogue between faiths. It became apparent as I worked with Nabil that his commitment to peace and justice is a driving force in his life. Wichita and the surrounding area - and the diverse faiths present there - are enhanced by the energy and commitment Nabil brings to the community.

Gary Flory, Director Kansas Institute for Peace and Conflict Resolution

As Nabil journeys through life, his entire being presents a clear expression of his understanding of the beliefs and teachings of Islam and how they relate to our struggling world. It is a gift to all of humanity to have Nabil's thoughts shared in this book.

Rev. Sam Muyskens, Executive Director Inter-Faith Ministries.

Nabil Seyam's partnership and leadership has helped law enforcement better understand and better serve the Muslim community

Gary Steed, Sedgwick County Sheriff

About the Author

Dr. Nabil Seyam is director of the Board of Administration of the Islamic Society of Wichita and cofounder of the Annoor Islamic School. He performs Friday sermons, marriage and divorce ceremonies, and death sermons. Dr. Seyam conducts marriage counseling and provides countless activities for Muslims and people of other faiths. He has done more than 300 speeches and interviews on politics, religion, peace-building, and multiculturalism throughout the state of Kansas. He was the recipient of the Leader of the Year in 2002 in Wichita and most recently was the recipient of the Community Servant Award by the University United Methodist Church in 2003. Dr. Seyam was selected for the Community Servant Award because of his active role in peace-building and multiculturalism throughout Kansas.

Dr. Seyam received his undergraduate degree in industrial engineering from Wichita State University and his master's and Ph.D. in safety engineering from Kennedy University. He is an adjunct instructor for Pittsburg State University and Wichita State University.

Dr. Seyam has served and is still serving on many boards, including those of the American Society of Safety Engineers, Wichita State University, Pittsburg State University, Newman University, Inter-Faith Ministries, Global Learning Center, Mayor Bob Knight's diversity task force, and the Child Care Association. His monthly writing on Islam is featured in the Q&A Times, and he has hosted a popular television series called ZYGO on public television station KPTS.

Besides his occupation as a corporate safety director and expert in the field of ergonomics, Dr. Seyam has been interviewed by reporters from CBS, ABC, NBC, radio stations and newspapers here and abroad about his perspective on such issues as politics and religion.

Dr. Seyam's personal relationship with many government officials (city, county, state, the governor, FBI, prisons, Highway Patrol.) has helped enhance the reputation of the Muslim community of Wichita. He is married and has six children.

Printed in the United States
22154LVS00005B/115-213